KV-194-782

ADVANCED ECONOMICS

THE M. & E. HANDBOOK SERIES

ADVANCED ECONOMICS

G. L. THIRKETTLE, B.Com.(Lond.), F.I.S.

Senior Lecturer, North Western Polytechnic

MACDONALD & EVANS LTD

8 John Street, London W.C.1

1968

First published May 1968
Reprinted February 1969
Reprinted May 1970

©

MACDONALD AND EVANS LTD
1968

S.B.N.: 7121 0114 4

*Printed in Great Britain
by Richard Clay (The Chaucer Press), Ltd.,
Bungay, Suffolk*

GENERAL INTRODUCTION

The HANDBOOK Series of Study Notes

HANDBOOKS are a new form of printed study notes designed to help students to prepare and revise for professional and other examinations. The books are carefully programmed so as to be self-contained courses of tuition in the subjects they cover. For this purpose they comprise detailed notes, self-testing questions and hints on examination technique.

HANDBOOKS can be used on their own or in conjunction with recommended textbooks. They are written by college lecturers, examiners and others with wide experience of students' difficulties and requirements. At all stages the main objective of the authors has been to prepare students for the practical business of passing examinations.

P. W. D. REDMOND
General Editor

NOTICE TO LECTURERS

Many lecturers are now using HANDBOOKS as working texts to save time otherwise wasted by students in protracted note-taking. The purpose of the series is to meet practical teaching requirements as far as possible, and lecturers are cordially invited to forward comments or criticisms to the Publishers for consideration.

AUTHOR'S PREFACE

THESE study notes are intended for use by students preparing for the *final examinations of professional bodies* who examine in the subject of economics. They deal in considerable detail with the theoretical aspects. They also cover most of the ground of the theory of first degree courses in economics. In conjunction with the progress tests they provide a self-contained course in economic analysis.

The book should also prove useful for revision, which must, of course, be a continuous process.

Necessary background. It is assumed that the student has already studied an intermediate course and covered the material such as is given in my *Basic Economics* (an M. & E. HANDBOOK to which this book forms a sequel). *The subject matter of that book will not therefore be repeated in this.*

The final syllabus of professional bodies includes "the subject matter of the intermediate syllabus in greater detail." It cannot be emphasised too strongly that *a thorough knowledge of the intermediate syllabus is a prerequisite of success at the final stage.* Too many students only just scrape through the intermediate and fail to rework the intermediate material before the final. Hence, particular attention should be paid to the revision of basic economics.

Method of study. First read the chapter being studied fairly quickly without paying attention to details in order to have an idea what it is all about. Then study the chapter, one paragraph at a time, until it is thoroughly understood. In some cases reference to your intermediate course may be necessary. Do not leave any chapter until you have checked whether you really know it, as distinct from having read about it. This is the purpose of the progress tests.

Progress tests. These are questionnaires at the end of each chapter. You should jot down answers and then check. A reference to the text is given in all cases. It is *not* sufficient to recognise that you have read about the matter dealt with in the question. Until you can answer the progress tests satisfactorily without reference to the notes you should not pass on to another chapter.

At this stage you should not rely upon one text-book, but should read as widely as time permits. A short bibliography is given in an appendix.

Review of previous study. Before starting on this Advanced Course, it is essential to revise all past work and, further, when reaching certain topics in this course to revise yet again what you learned about them in your intermediate course. Indications are given throughout this advanced course when this should be done.

The fundamental knowledge you should posess before attempting this course is contained in *Basic Economics*, to which reference is made from time to time.

The matters which should be thoroughly known are:

(1) *The nature of economics and economic activity :* that economics is a science, uses scientific methods and deals with that aspect of man's behaviour when faced with scarcity; that economic activity takes the form of production, changing resources into the form required for consumption; that in real life economic problems are bound up with questions of policy, justice, morality and the level of intelligence of the people.

(2) *The national income* regarded as three aspects of the total of goods and services produced, namely, (a) the national income, (b) the national product and (c) the national expenditure.

(3) *The law of diminishing marginal productivity* and *the law of increasing costs* which follows from it.

(4) *The determination of price.* To say that this is determined by supply and demand invites the question what determines supply and demand. This will vary according to whether there is perfect competition, imperfect competition, monopoly, whether we are concerned with the short-run price or the long-run price, and much more.

(5) *The distribution of the national income in the form of wages, interest, profit and rent*

(6) *Money*, distinguishing its static functions from the dynamic one of helping to control the level of economic activity (the question of monetary policy); its creation and control by the banking system and the government.

(7) *International trade and the balance of payments.*

(8) *Public finance*; the aims of taxation, its principles, the kinds of taxes and their incidence.

Acknowledgements. I thank the Chartered Institute of Secretaries and the Senate of the University of London for permission to reproduce past examination questions.

G. L. T.

March, 1968

CONTENTS

LIST OF FIGURES

CHAPTER I

THE INDIFFERENCE CURVE TECHNIQUE

1. Indifference curves. The fundamental economic problem of choice, whether to have X or Y or so much of X and so much of Y, how to divide one's time between leisure and work, the question of how much to consume (income now) and how much to save (income in the future), can usefully be analysed by means of indifference curves.

Let us consider a person who has 4 units of commodity X and 1 unit of commodity Y. He will obtain a certain amount of satisfaction from this combination of goods. Now consider, if he only has 3 units of commodity X, how many units will he require of commodity Y in order to obtain the same amount of satisfaction from the new combination? Let us suppose 2 units. Then it would be possible to say that this person was indifferent to 4 units of X *plus* 1 unit of Y or 3 units of X *plus* 2 units of Y. He obtained the same amount of satisfaction from either combination.

Note that the question of measuring satisfaction does not arise; all that is required is the ability to state whether one combination is preferable to another or whether the combinations give equal satisfaction; that is, the consumer is indifferent as to which combination he has.

Below are four combinations; our consumer is quite indifferent as to which of the four he has.

Combination	Commodity X		Commodity Y	Substitution of Y for X
1	4 units	*plus*	1 unit	—
2	3 units	*plus*	2 units	1 unit
3	2 units	*plus*	4 units	2 units
4	1 unit	*plus*	7 units	3 units

Comparing combinations 1 and 2, it is seen that 1 more unit of Y compensates for the loss of 1 unit of X. However, comparing combinations 2 and 3, it is seen that 2 units of Y are now necessary to compensate for the loss of one additional unit

1

of X. In the next combination 3 units of Y are required to compensate for a further additional loss of one unit of X.

As the amount of X becomes smaller, and the amount of Y greater, so X becomes more and more significant and Y less and less significant; hence more and more of Y is required to compensate for the loss of successive units of X.

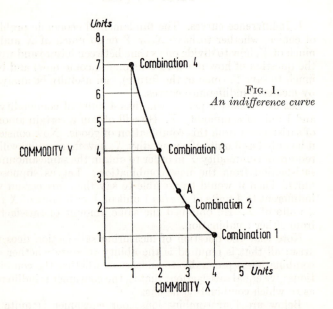

Fig. 1.
An indifference curve

In Fig. 1, the four combinations have been plotted on a graph. The points denoting the combinations have been joined by a smooth curve. This curve is an *indifference curve*. All points on this curve show combinations of X and Y which give equal satisfaction. The point marked A shows that $2\frac{1}{2}$ units of Y *plus* $2\frac{2}{3}$ units of X would give the same amount of satisfaction as the other combinations plotted. (The units of the commodities are assumed to be divisible.)

2. Indifference maps. Let us now consider four more combinations. This time each combination is preferable to any of the four previous combinations. The first, for example, contains more of both *X and Y* than the corresponding combination of the previous group.

Combination	Commodity X	Commodity Y	Substitution of Y for X
1	6	2	—
2	5	4	2
3	4	7	3
4	3	11	4

And as before, in return for each successive loss of one unit of *X*, an increasing amount of commodity *Y* is required to compensate. In Fig. 2 the second group of combinations have been plotted and have been joined by a smooth curve. This

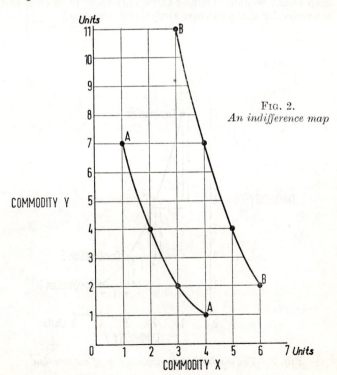

Fig. 2.
An indifference map

has given a second indifference curve which has been marked
B. The first indifference curve has been repeated and this is
marked *A*. Any combination on curve *B* is preferable to any
combination on curve *A*; curve *B* is a higher indifference
curve than *A*. The farther the indifference curve is from the
origin (marked *O*), the higher it is; the higher the indifference
curve the greater the amount of satisfaction obtained. It
would be possible to draw up a whole series of tables such as
those given above in respect of the *same* consumer. It would
consequently be possible to get a whole series of indifference
curves. Such a series of indifference curves constitutes an
indifference map.

There are, in reality, an infinite number of indifference
curves on an indifference map, but if they were all shown, the
map would be unintelligible; hence only those of interest and
relevance for any particular analysis are shown.

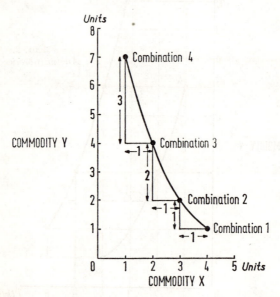

Fig. 3.—*The diminishing marginal rate of substitution*

Indifference curves are analogous to contours. But whereas contours can indicate actual heights, indifference curves cannot show "heights" of satisfaction; all that can be said is that a higher indifference curve denotes greater satisfaction than a lower one, but how much greater it is impossible to measure.

3. The marginal rate of substitution. Figure 3 shows the same indifference curve as in Fig. 1. From this we can see, starting with combination 4 at the top, that the consumer will substitute 1 unit of X for 3 units of Y. This is the *marginal rate of substitution* of X for Y. It is the ratio in which X is substituted for Y without the consumer being either better or worse off. Going from combination 3 to combination 2, the consumer will now substitute for a further unit of X only 2 units of Y. The marginal rate of substitution of X for Y is lower. It will be seen that as the stock of X increases and Y decreases, the marginal rate of substitution falls.

The Law of Diminishing Marginal Rate of Substitution states that:

The marginal rate of substitution of X for Y diminishes as the amount of X possessed increases and the amount of Y decreases.

The marginal rate of substitution is measured by the slope of the indifference curve.

4. The properties of indifference curves. These are:

(*a*) *Indifference curves are convex to the origin.* This follows from the law of diminishing marginal rate of substitution (*see* **3** above). The curve becomes steeper and steeper as the consumer moves upwards along the curve (*see* Fig. 3).

(*b*) *An indifference curve has a negative slope.* It slopes down from left to right. As the quantity of Y decreases, the quantity of X *must* increase; otherwise it would mean that the same quantity of X and different quantities of Y would be equally desirable.

(*c*) *Indifference curves cannot intersect.* We prove this by the *reductio ad absurdum* method. We assume they can intersect and then show that this assumption leads to an absurd conclusion. Refer to Fig. 4 and let I_1 and I_2 be two indifference curves which intersect at Z. This point represents RZ of X *plus* LZ of Y. This combination is equal to OM of X *plus* MN of Y (at point N on indifference curve I_1)

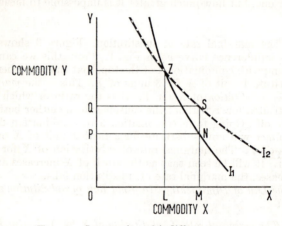

FIG. 4.—*Intersection of indifference curves*

or OM of X *plus* MS of Y (at point S on indifference curve I_2). It follows that MN of Y is equal to MS of Y. But MS is preferable to MN. Indifference curves cannot, therefore, intersect.

PROGRESS TEST 1

1. What is the law of the diminishing marginal rate of substitution? (3)

2. What is the marginal rate of substitution and how is it measured? (3)

3. What is (a) an indifference curve, (b) an indifference map? (1, 2)

4. What is meant by saying that an indifference curve has a negative slope? (4(b))

5. Why has an indifference curve a negative slope? (4(b))

6. In what ways do indifference curves resemble, and in what ways do they differ from, contours? (2)

7. What are the characteristics of indifference curves? (4)

8. What is meant by being on a higher indifference curve? (2)

9. What is meant by saying indifference curves are convex to the origin? (4)

10. What method would you use to analyse a consumer's choice between two commodities? (1)

11. Can indifference curves intersect? Give the reason for your answer. (4)

CHAPTER II

THE THEORY OF DEMAND

1. The price line. The tastes of an individual are shown by means of his indifference curves and changes in tastes are shown by changes in these curves (*see* **4** below; also Fig. 8). But *demand* depends not only on a *subjective scale of preferences* but also on the *objective facts of income and prices*. These are shown in Fig. 5. Along the *Y* axis is shown the amount of

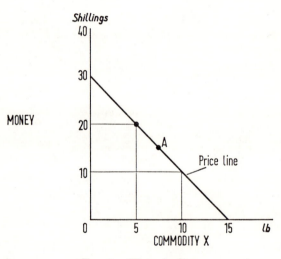

Fig. 5.—*The price line*

income—in the case illustrated this is 30*s*. Along the *X* axis is shown units of commodity *X*. If the whole of the income was spent on this commodity, 15 *lb* would be purchased. The line joining the points denoting the 30*s*. and the 15 *lb* is the price line.

8

The price line shows:

(a) *The price of the commodity.* This is given by the *slope* of the price line. In the example given the price of the commodity is 30*s.* divided by 15 *lb, i.e.* 2*s.* per *lb.*

(b) *The combinations of income and commodity X it is possible to have.* Any point on the price line will indicate this, *e.g.* the point marked *A* (Fig. 5) denotes that it is possible to have 15*s.* income and $7\frac{1}{2}$ *lb* of *X.* 15*s.* has been spent purchasing $7\frac{1}{2}$ *lb* of commodity *X,* leaving 15*s.* income unspent.

(c) *The income of the consumer.* This is denoted by the point where the price line cuts the *Y* axis.

NOTE: An alternative name for the price line is the budget line.

2. Price change and the price line. Referring to Fig. 6 it can be seen that the price line P_3 denotes a price of *OC* divided by OM_3 and price line P_2 denotes a price of *OC* divided by OM_2. But, since OM_3 is greater than OM_2, it follows that the

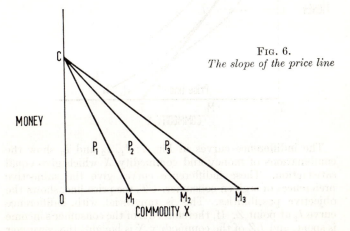

FIG. 6.
The slope of the price line

price denoted by price line P_3 is less than the price denoted by P_2. Similarly it can be shown that the price denoted by price line P_1 is higher still. *The greater the slope the higher the price.*

3. The determination of an individual's demand. The indifference curves described in Chapter I showed the consumer's
preferences between X and Y. The choice in real life is not
between two goods; how much of X and how much of Y. The
choice is how much of each of a multiplicity of goods and
services. We can still, however, use the indifference curve
technique. One commodity or service, say X, is plotted along
the X axis as in Fig. 7. All the other goods and services com-
peting for the consumer's income are plotted along the Y axis.
The only way in which all the other goods and services can be
added together is to add their money values, which means
knowing their prices. The addition will be a sum of money;
this is plotted along the Y axis.

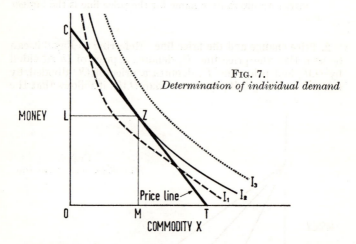

Fig. 7.
Determination of individual demand

The indifference curves in Fig. 7: I_1, I_2 and I_3 show the
combinations of money and commodity X which give equal
satisfaction. These indifference curves give the subjective
preferences of a given consumer. CT, the price line, shows the
objective possibilities. This is tangential with indifference
curve I_2 at point Z. If, therefore, CL of the consumer's income
is spent, and LZ of the commodity X is bought, the consumer
is on the highest indifference curve he can reach. That is, by
buying this amount of X he obtains more satisfaction than if
he had bought any other quantity.

THE THEORY OF DEMAND 「1

Given then:

(a) *A scale of preferences*, denoted by a series of indifference curves (I_1, I_2, I_3 in Fig. 7).
(b) *Income*, denoted where price line cuts Y axis (OC in Fig. 7).
(c) *Price of the commodity*, denoted by the slope of the price line (OC divided by OT in Fig. 7), the individual's demand is determined (LZ in Fig. 7). By adding the individual demands (each individual will have his own indifference map and income) the total demand is obtained.

When a consumer is on the highest possible indifference curve we can say that the marginal rate of substitution between income and commodity X is equal to the price of X. The marginal rate of substitution is the slope of the tangent of an indifference curve (*see* I, 3) and this same slope is the price of X (*see* 1 above). Similarly, we can say that the marginal rate of substitution between income and commodity Y is equal to the price of Y. It follows that a consumer demands those quantities of commodities which make the marginal rate of substitution between them proportional to their prices. He could not increase his satisfaction by buying more of one good and less of another.

4. Changes in scales of preference. Changes in the scale of preferences of a consumer are shown by changes in the position of his indifference curves. This is illustrated in Fig. 8. The broken lines indicate a series of indifference curves and Z_1 the point of equilibrium—the point where subjective preferences and objective possibilities coincide. A_1Z_1 is the amount of commodity X that is purchased.

An increased preference for X has the effect of increasing the steepness of the curves as indicated by the other series of indifference curves denoted by the unbroken lines. The marginal rate of substitution of X for money is higher throughout the curve than before. Z_2 is the new point of equilibrium, and A_2Z_2 is the new amount of X that is now bought. More of X is bought and less of other commodities. Income and prices remained unchanged.

5. Changes in income. If income increases but the price of commodity X remains unchanged, then the price line will have

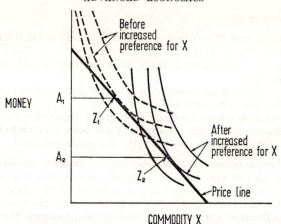

COMMODITY X

FIG. 8.—*Changes in scales of preference*

the same slope but will cut the Y axis at a higher point. This is shown in Fig. 9. I_1T_1 is the price line when income is OI_1, I_2T_2 is the price line when OI_2 is the income, I_3T_3 is the price line when OI_3 is the income and so on. All these price lines are parallel since the price is unchanged—they have the same slope.

The effect of an increased income is that the consumer attains a position of equilibrium on a higher indifference curve. When the income was OI_1 the equilibrium point was M_1; when income was OI_2, the equilibrium point was M_2 and so on. The line joining points M_1, M_2, M_3, etc., is known as the *income-consumption curve* and shows for each income the amount of commodity that is bought. For example, with income OT_1, the amount is A_1M_1; with income OT_2, the demand is A_2M_2.

6. The case of "inferior" goods. It does not necessarily follow that an increased income will give rise to an increased demand for a particular commodity. Such a case is illustrated in Fig. 10. Here we see that as the income of the consumer increases from OA_1 to OA_2 the demand for commodity X falls from A_1M_1 to A_2M_2. This is not a very frequent case. But such goods are known as "inferior" goods—goods that a consumer only buys when his income is low.

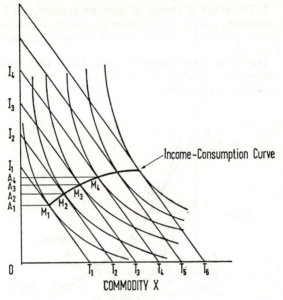

Fig. 9.—*Changes in income*

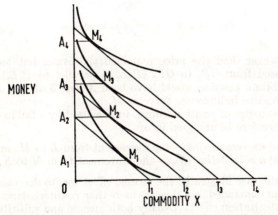

Fig. 10.—*Income effect on demand for "inferior" goods*

7. The effect of change of price on demand. In Fig. 11 the consumer's original equilibrium position is shown at point L. This is for income and price denoted by price line P_1L_1 (*see* **1** above).

The fall in price denoted by P_1L_3 (*see* **2** above) changes the consumer's equilibrium position to N. In this position he would buy more of X.

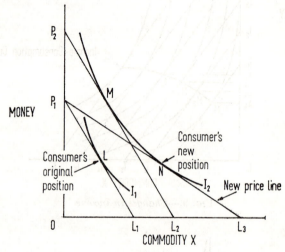

FIG. 11.—*The effect of price change*

However, had the price remained the same, but income increased from OP_1 to OP_2 (P_2L_2 is parallel to P_1L_1), the equilibrium position would have been M (*see* **5** above). N is on the same indifference curve as M.

The change of position from L to N caused by a fall in price can therefore be analysed into:

    (*a*) *an income effect*—the movement from L to M; and
    (*b*) *a substitution effect*—the movement from M to N.

In the case illustrated the income effect was to decrease the amount demanded, but this was more than counterbalanced by the substitution effect. Usually both income and substitution effect increase the demand as the price falls.

8. The price–consumption curve. As the price of a commodity falls it is a general rule that more will be bought. This is exemplified in Fig. 12. As the price falls, indicated by the lessening of the slope of the price line, so the amount bought increases, indicated by the equilibrium points E_1, E_2 ... E_6 (the points of tangency of price lines and indifference curves) moving to the right. The line joining the points E_1, E_2,

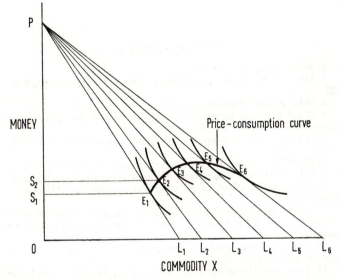

FIG. 12.—*The price–consumption curve*

E_3 ... E_6 is a *price–consumption curve*. It shows the relationship between the amount spent and the quantity bought. When price is denoted by the line PL_1, the quantity bought is S_1E_1 and the amount spent is PS_1; when price is denoted by PL_2, the quantity bought is S_2E_2 and the amount spent is PS_2.

It would be possible to draw a demand curve from this indifference map. OP divided by OL_1 gives a price and the quantity bought at this price is denoted by the position of E_1; this is one point on the demand curve. Similarly, all the other points on the demand curve could be ascertained.

It will be noted from Fig. 12 that, although the quantity bought increases as the price is less, the amount spent on the commodity first decreases (less income is exchanged for commodity X), then remains constant over a certain price range, and then increases. The demand in this particular example is first inelastic, then of unit elasticity and finally elastic.

PROGRESS TEST 2

1. What is a price line? (1)
2. What determines an individual's demand for a commodity? (3)
3. What is an inferior good? (6)
4. What is meant by (a) the income effect, (b) the substitution effect, of a fall in price? (7)
5. How does a price–consumption curve show the elasticity of demand? (8)
6. How does a price line show the price of a commodity? (1)
7. What is the effect of a change in price upon the price line? (2)
8. What is the effect of a change of income upon the price line? (5)
9. If A's taste for a certain commodity lessened, what would be the effect upon his indifference map, income and prices remaining unchanged? (4)
10. Compare an income–consumption curve and a price–consumption curve. (5, 8)
11. How are the subjective tastes of an individual and the objective facts of his income and prices brought into equilibrium? (1, 3)
12. What is the relationship between the marginal rate of substitution between two commodities and their prices? (3)
13. When using the indifference curve technique of analysis how are (a) the income of the consumer, (b) the price of a commodity, (c) the preferences of the consumer shown? (1)
14. On a graph, show price lines relating to different incomes, but in respect of the same price. (5)
15. On a graph, show price lines relating to different prices, but in respect of the same income. Indicate which would be the lowest price. (2)
16. What determines the indifference curve which a person reaches, given his income and the price of the commodity he is purchasing? (3)

17. Show by means of a suitable diagram that an increase in income may, for a given commodity:

(a) Increase the demand.
(b) Decrease the demand.
(c) Keep the demand constant. **(5)**

CHAPTER III

FURTHER CONSIDERATIONS ON ELASTICITY

Revision of basic study on elasticity is essential before reading this chapter

1. Arc elasticity of demand. Changes in prices (and consequent changes in demand) in a real economy are not infinitesimally small and hence the measurement of elasticity is over an appreciable price interval (as distinct from the theoretical concept of elasticity at a price). Such elasticity is known as *arc elasticity*.

One way of measuring the elasticity of demand for a commodity is to consider the effect on the revenue derived from its sale. In Fig. 13 we consider the arc elasticity of demand over the price interval P_1 to P_2. At 2s. the demand is 10 *lb*; total

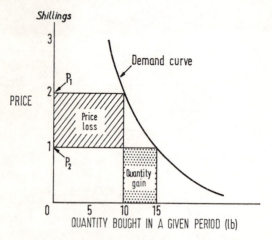

FIG. 13.—*The effect on revenue of elasticity*

revenue 20*s*. At 1*s*. the demand is 15 *lb*; total revenue 15*s*. The difference in revenue, namely 5*s*., can be analysed as follows:

Price loss—the loss due to a lower price. 10 *lb* at 1*s*. = 10*s*.
Quantity gain—gain due to selling a greater quantity. 5 *lb* at 1*s*. = 5*s*.

Since the price loss is greater than the quantity gain the demand is inelastic over this price range. If they are equal the demand has unit elasticity. If the price loss is less than the quantity gain, the demand is elastic.

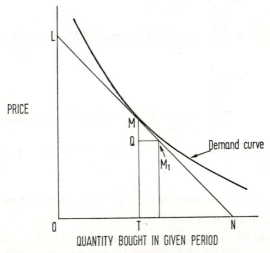

Fig. 14.—*Measurement of point elasticity*

2. Point elasticity—its measurement. Theoretically elasticity should be measured *at* a particular price since elasticity changes with price. In Fig. 14, *M* is the point on the demand curve which denotes the amount demanded *at* price *TM*. It is required to measure the elasticity *at* this price. *LN* is tangential to the demand curve at point *M*.

Elasticity is measured by dividing the proportional change in quantity by the proportional change in price when both these changes QM_1 are infinitesimally small.

$$\text{Elasticity} = \frac{QM_1 \text{ (increase in quantity)}}{OT \text{ (original quantity)}} \text{ divided by}$$

$$\frac{QM \text{ (fall in price)}}{TM \text{ (original price)}}$$

$$= \frac{QM_1}{OT} \times \frac{TM}{QM} = \frac{QM_1}{QM} \times \frac{TM}{OT}$$

$$= \frac{TN}{TM} \times \frac{TM}{OT}$$

$$\left(\frac{QM_1}{QM} = \frac{TN}{TM} \text{ since } MQM_1 \text{ and } MTN \text{ are similar tri-} \atop \text{angles} \right)$$

$$= \frac{TN}{OT}$$

$$= \frac{NM}{ML} \quad \text{(since } MTN \text{ and } LON \text{ are similar tri-angles)}$$

As the increase in quantity becomes infinitesimally small, M_1 approaches M, becoming coincidental at the point of tangentcy.

The elasticity at point $M = \dfrac{NM}{ML}$, LN being tangential to the demand curve at M.

It will be noted that the elasticity is negative, since increases in price are accompanied by decreases in quantity, and vice versa. Also note that the elasticity is *not* the slope of LN.

Elasticity numerically greater than -1 (*e.g.* -3) is *elastic*.

Elasticity numerically less than -1 (*e.g.* $-\cdot8$) is *inelastic*.

Elasticity equal to -1 is *unit elasticity*.

3. Price, marginal revenue and elasticity. There is a precise relationship between these three quantities. Refer to Fig. 15.

At point P on the demand curve the price is MP and the marginal revenue is MR.

The revenue when price is MP is MP (price) $\times$ OM (quantity) which equals the area $TOMP$. The revenue is also

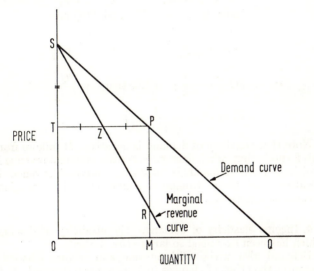

Fig. 15.—*Elasticity, marginal revenue and price*

the sum of all the marginal revenues which equals the area $SOMR$.

$$TOMP = SOMR$$
$$\therefore \ TOMP - OMRZT = SOMR - OMRZT$$
$$\therefore \ RPZ = STZ$$

These triangles are equal:

hence $\qquad\qquad TS = RP$ and $TZ = ZP$......... (1)

also $\qquad\qquad \dfrac{TS}{TP} = \dfrac{MP}{MQ}$ (triangles STP and PMQ are similar) .... (2)

Marginal revenue $MR = MP - RP = MP - TS$ $\qquad$ (1)

$$= MP - \frac{MP \times TP}{MQ} \qquad (2)$$

$$= MP \left(1 - \frac{TP}{MQ}\right)$$

$$= MP \left(1 - \frac{OM}{MQ}\right) = MP \left(1 - \frac{SP}{PQ}\right)$$

[since triangles PMQ and SOQ are similar.]

$$= MP \left(1 + \frac{PS}{PQ}\right) \qquad [SP = -PS]$$

$$= MP \left(1 + \frac{1}{E}\right) \quad \left[\text{Elasticity} = \frac{PQ}{PS}\right]$$

$$= Price \left(1 + \frac{1}{Elasticity}\right)$$

Note that elasticity of demand is negative. It follows from this formula that, when demand is elastic, marginal revenue is positive; when demand is inelastic, marginal revenue is negative; and when demand has unit elasticity, marginal revenue is zero (*see* 2).

4. Income elasticity of demand. The elasticity of demand which has been examined so far is *price elasticity*.

Demand also varies with income and income elasticity measures the effect of changes in income upon demand. It is defined as follows: *Income elasticity is proportionate change in demand divided by proportionate change in income.* For example: with an income of £1000 per year A bought 4 bottles of beer per week. When his income rose to £1200 per year he bought 5 bottles.

$$\text{Income elasticity of demand} = \frac{5 - 4}{4} \div \frac{1200 - 1000}{1000} = 1\tfrac{1}{4}$$

Unlike price elasticity, which is almost invariably negative, income elasticity is generally positive. "Inferior" goods have a negative income elasticity.

5. Cross-elasticity of demand. This measures the effect on demand when the price of a substitute changes. It is defined as follows: *Cross-elasticity is proportionate change in demand for X divided by proportionate change in price of Y.* For example:

An increase in the price of apples from 2s. per *lb* to 2s. 8d. caused A to buy more pears, 5 *lb* instead of 4.

The cross-elasticity of demand for pears with respect to the prices of apples

$$= \frac{5 - 4}{4} \div \frac{2s.\ 8d. - 2s.}{2s.} = \tfrac{3}{4}$$

If the cross-elasticity of demand for pears with respect to the prices of oranges were, say, $\tfrac{1}{2}$ it would mean that pears would be a better substitute for apples than for oranges. The higher the cross-elasticity of demand the better the substitutes.

NOTE: It is possible to define a monopoly in terms of cross-elasticities. It is a firm, the cross-elasticity of demand of whose product with respect to the prices of every other product is small.

PROGRESS TEST 3

1. Distinguish between arc and point elasticity. (**1, 2**)
2. How is point elasticity measured? (**2**)
3. Define (*a*) income, (*b*) cross-elasticity. (**4, 5**)
4. What is the relation between marginal revenue and elasticity? If marginal revenue is zero, what is the elasticity? (**3**)
5. If price loss is greater than quantity gain, is the demand elastic or inelastic? (**1**)
6. Is price elasticity negative or positive? (**2**)
7. Is income elasticity negative or positive? (**4**)
8. What does a high figure of cross elasticity mean? (**5**)
9. Marginal revenue is 8s. Price elasticity is -0.5. What is the price? (**3**)
10. If XYZ Ltd. produces a commodity X and the cross-elasticity of demand for X with respect to the prices of all other commodities is small, what can you say about XYZ Ltd.? (**5**)

CHAPTER IV

THE THEORY OF PRODUCTION

1. Factors of production. These consist of:

(*a*) Human resources.
(*b*) Non-human *tangible* resources.

These provide the *inputs* which the process of production turns into *outputs* of goods and services. It is the *services* of the factors that are required and whether they are actually employed will depend upon:

(*a*) The market demands for their services.
(*b*) The valuations of factor owners regarding income and leisure.

There are endless kinds of factors of production; if they are incomplete substitutes they are separate factors of production. If they are completely substitutable—in terms of constant product curves (*see* **2**) if the marginal rate of substitution between them is always unity—they are the same factor of production.

Factors may be:

(*a*) *Specific*, only capable of being used for producing one particular type of output.
(*b*) *Non-specific*, capable of being used for producing many different kinds of output.

A further classification of factors is as follows:

(*a*) *Fixed factors*. These are the factors whose quantity and hence their cost cannot be changed until a certain time (known as the short-run) has elapsed. Machinery whose cost (interest on investment in it and depreciation) is constant over a large range of output.
(*b*) *Variable factors*. These are factors whose quantity and hence cost varies with output. Examples of this are labour and materials.

2. Constant product curves. Refer to Fig. 16. Quantities of factor X are drawn along one axis and quantities of factor Y along the other. Suppose a certain quantity of goods can be produced with a certain amount of X and a certain amount of Y, marked on the diagram by point A. Suppose further, that the *same* quantity of goods can be produced by using more of X but less of Y, marked on the diagram at point B. A large number of points could be indicated showing various combinations of factors X and Y which would produce the same quantity of output. The line joining all these points is a *constant product curve* (also known as an *equal product curve* or *isoquant*).

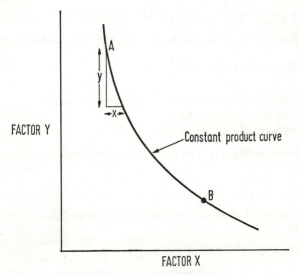

Fig. 16.—*Constant product curve*

A constant product curve is analogous to an indifference curve, factors X and Y replace commodities X and Y. Like an indifference curve, a constant product curve is convex to the origin. As more of factor X is used and less of factor Y, increasing amounts of X are required to compensate for the loss of Y. The marginal rate of substitution between the factors (y/x) diminishes.

This is another formulation of the *law of diminishing marginal productivity*. By using more of X with the same amount of Y, output would be increased. If, now, an *equal* amount of *increase in output* is required, an *increase in the amount of additional X* would be necessary. Equal increments in the amount of X would mean diminishing increases in output.

3. The minimum cost condition. Consider Fig. 17. The slope at point $Z = y/x$ which is the marginal rate of substitution between the factors. Let the total output be decreased by one unit when y units less of factor Y is used; then

$$y = \frac{1}{\text{Marginal product of } Y} \cdot$$

If x units more of X is now used the output is increased by 1 unit and x is therefore equal to $\dfrac{1}{\text{Marginal product of } X} \cdot$

$$\frac{y}{x} = \frac{1}{\text{Marginal product of } Y} \div \frac{1}{\text{Marginal product of } X}$$

$$= \frac{\text{Marginal product of } X}{\text{Marginal product of } Y}$$

Refer to Fig. 17. The price line indicates the combinations of factors Y and X that can be purchased for a given outlay. If the whole of the expenditure is spent on factor Y, OY units will be bought. If all is spent on X, OX units will be bought.

Cost of OY units of Y = Cost of OX units of X = Expenditure.

$$\text{The slope of the price line} = \frac{OY}{OX} = \frac{\text{Expenditure}}{\text{Cost of 1 unit of } Y}$$

$$\text{divided by } \frac{\text{Expenditure}}{\text{Cost of 1 unit of } X} = \frac{\text{Cost of 1 unit of } X}{\text{Cost of 1 unit of } Y}$$

At point L, the price line indicates OM of X and OP of Y; the total cost will be the same as any other combination on the price line.

Still referring to Fig. 17, at Z, the price line (whose slope gives the marginal cost of X divided by the marginal cost of Y) is tangential to the constant product curve. This is the highest output obtainable with the expenditure of the

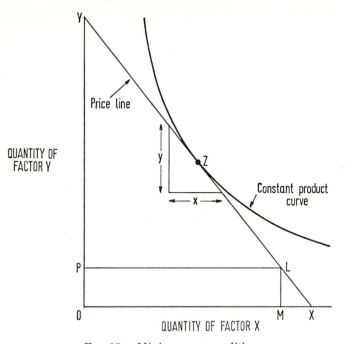

FIG. 17.—*Minimum cost condition*

tangential price line. The slope of the constant product curve at

$$Z = \frac{y}{x} = \frac{\text{Marginal product of } X}{\text{Marginal product of } Y}$$

$$= \frac{\text{Marginal cost of } X}{\text{Marginal cost of } Y}$$

This conclusion can relate to any number of factors and states that factors of production are used in those proportions which make their marginal products proportional to their marginal costs. The cost per unit of output will then be at a minimum.

4. The least outlay curve. Figure 18 shows a number of price lines, all parallel, and hence the relative prices of factors X and

Y are the same. However, each shows a different total expenditure on these factors.

Each price line will be tangential to a constant product curve, *e.g.* price line PL is tangential to the constant product curve whose output is 1000 units at point Z. Point Z gives the cheapest method of producing 1000 units, *viz.* OM of factor X and OQ of factor Y.

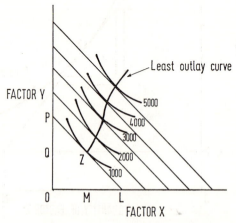

FIG. 18.—*Least outlay curve*

If all the points of tangency are joined by a line, a *least outlay curve* is drawn. It shows the cheapest method of combining the factors to produce any given output. Hence, it shows how the proportions of the factors used might be altered as the firm grows. For example, in Fig. 18 the proportions of factors X and Y used to produce an output of 4000 units at lowest cost are different from the proportions of these factors used to produce 1000 units at the lowest cost.

5. Returns to scale. In Fig. 19 the least outlay curve, labelled scale line, is a straight line starting from the origin. Constant product curves are shown increasing by 100 units.

Since the scale line is straight, the proportion of factors X and Y remains unchanged, *viz.* 4 units of factor Y, and 3 units of factor X. Thus, when output increases from 100 units to 200 units, the increase in factor Y is 1·2 units and the increase in factor X is ·9 units. Increase in output from 200 units to 300 units requires an increase in factor Y of ·8 units and an increase in factor X of ·6 units. Both factors increase in the same proportion.

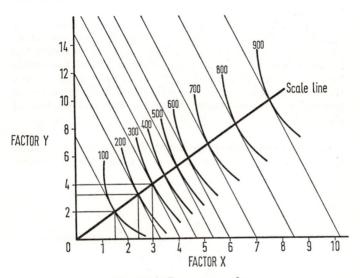

FIG. 19.—*Returns to scale*

It will be seen that, from 100 to 300 units of output, the additional quantities of factors used diminish with each increase of 100 units in output—the points where the constant product curves and the price lines cut are getting closer together; the increase in expenditure on factors diminishes for each additional increase of 100 units of output. The firm is working under *increasing returns to scale*—each additional increase in output of 100 units costs less.

From 300 to 600 units of output, the additional quantities of factors required for each additional 100 units of output remain constant—the points where the constant product curve and the price lines intersect are the same distance apart. The firm is working under *constant returns to scale*—each additional increase in output of 100 units costs the same.

From 600 units and onwards, the additional quantities of factors required for each additional 100 units of output increase—the points where the constant product curves and the price lines intersect get farther and farther apart—the firm is working under *diminishing returns to scale*—each additional increase in output of 100 units costs more.

The scale line enables the question of the scale of operations and the question of the proportions in which the factors are to be used to be separated. When, however, the least outlay line is not straight, as in Fig. 20, it is much more difficult to separate these questions. It is possible, however, to separate roughly the two problems—bends in the line itself indicate change in proportions and movement along the line is indicative of changes in scale.

6. Fixed factors and outlay curves. Least outlay curves show the least cost combination on the assumption that the factors

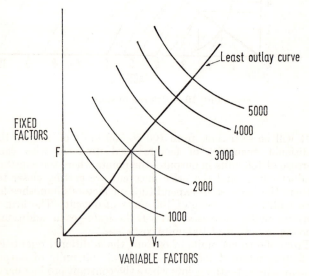

Fig. 20.—*Fixed factors and the outlay curve*

are freely variable. In the short run, certain factors are not variable, giving rise to fixed costs.

However, the technique can be used to show the output which will give the lowest average costs. In Fig. 20, OF shows the quantity of fixed factors. An output of 2000, using OV of variable factors, will give the lowest average cost per unit of output.

For an output of something over 2000 units of output with the same amount of fixed factors, using OV_1 of the variable factors, the cost per unit of output would be higher—point L does not lie on the least outlay curve. The firm would not be working at its optimum output.

7. Elasticity of substitution. The marginal rate of substitution varies with the proportion of the factors of production (or commodities) (*see* Fig. 3). Figure 21 shows the marginal rate of substitution plotted against ratios of factors (or commodities). The resulting curve is the *marginal rate of substitution curve*.

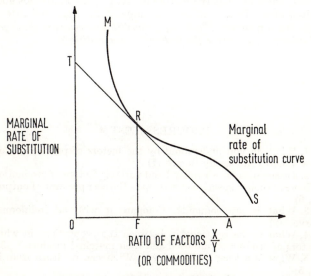

Fig. 21.—*Elasticity of substitution*

The elasticity of substitution measures the responsiveness of the marginal rate of substitution to changes in the proportion of the factors (or commodities).

It is measured by the proportional change in the proportion of the factors (or commodities) divided by the proportional change in the marginal rate of substitution. The changes are measured along an indifference curve in the case of commodities and along a constant product curve in the case of factors of production.

In order to find the elasticity of substitution for any given ratio of factors (or commodities), a tangent is drawn to the marginal rate of substitution curve, as at R in Fig. 21. The ratio of the factors (or commodities) at this point is OF and the marginal rate of substitution is ER. The elasticity of substitution is AR/RT. (This is exactly how the elasticity of demand is measured, given the demand curve.)

When the marginal rate of substitution curve is flat, the elasticity of substitution is very high, so that the factors (or commodities) are very good substitutes. When the marginal rate of substitution curve is steep, the elasticity of substitution is low, showing that the factors (or commodities) are not good substitutes. This explains the shape of the marginal rate of substitution curve. *Elasticity of substitution measures the degree of substitution between the factors (or commodities).*

PROGRESS TEST 4

1. What do you understand by the factors of production and how would you classify them? (1)

2. Distinguish between fixed and variable factors of production. What are their respective effects upon the cost per unit of output? (1, 6)

3. What is an isoquant? Compare it with an indifference curve. (2)

4. What is the relationship between the proportions in which factors of production are used and their marginal products? (3)

5. What is a least outlay curve? What can we learn from it? (4, 5)

6. What is elasticity of substitution and how is it measured? (7)

7. Given a scale line how would you determine whether the firm was working under (a) diminishing, (b) constant or (c) increasing returns to scale. (5)

8. What does the elasticity of substitution measure? (7)

9. Given a marginal rate of substitution curve, how would you measure the elasticity of substitution at any given point? (7)

10. Show how factors of production must be combined in order that the cost of production per unit of output shall be at a minimum. (3)

CHAPTER V

COST AND SUPPLY

1. Cost and size of output. Costs may fall as size of output increases for the following reasons:

(a) Indivisibilities

(i) *Technical indivisibilities.* Machinery is only available in certain sizes. In some cases complicated machinery (computers and automation) is only practicable when very large outputs are required. These lead to alternating stages of increasing and decreasing returns to scale.

(ii) *Selling indivisibilities.* National advertising is a good example.

(iii) *Research indivisibilities.*

(b) Specialisation. There are limitations to increase in efficiency due to specialisation. When a man is fully occupied on one particular job a bigger output does not lead to further economies in that direction. Although management can only be fully used in a large firm, sooner or later, diseconomies will arise because of the difficulties of co-ordination and decision-making.

2. Supply in the short period. The costs of a firm in the short-run (*see* IV, 1) when certain factors are fixed are shown in Fig. 22. Note particularly that the marginal cost curve cuts both the total average cost curve and the average variable cost curve at their lowest points. (*See Basic Economics*, Chap. IX.)

Figure 23 shows the short-run cost curves of a firm. In competitive conditions the firm is a price-taker (its output being small in comparison to the total supply, it has negligible effect on the price) and the diagram indicates the outputs of the firm when faced with the various market prices.

When price is OP_1, the output of the firm would be OT_1 to equate marginal cost and marginal revenue. This output would give the firm a smaller loss than at any other output, but

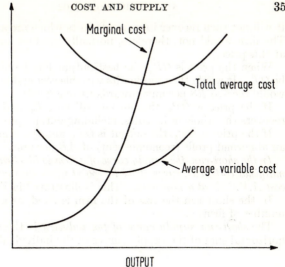

FIG. 22.—*Short-run costs of a firm*

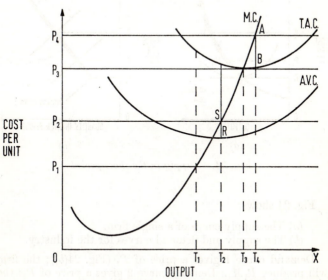

FIG. 23.—*Firm's output in short-run*

it will not then recover its variable costs which are avoidable. The firm would not, therefore, normally produce any output at this price.

When the price is OP_2, the best output for the firm would be OT_2. It would then recover its variable cost and in addition would receive RS per unit towards its overheads.

If the price is OP_3, the output will be OT_3, and the firm recovers the whole of its costs, including normal profit.

If the price is OP_4, the output is OT_4, and the firm receives an abnormal profit (economic rent) of AB per unit.

In the short-run, the supply curve of a firm is identical with the marginal cost M.C. curve above the point where average variable cost A.V.C. is at a minimum. This is illustrated in Fig. 24(a).

In the short-run the size of the firm is fixed, as is also the number of firms.

The *short-run supply curve of the industry* is therefore the horizontal sum of the supply curves of the individual firms.

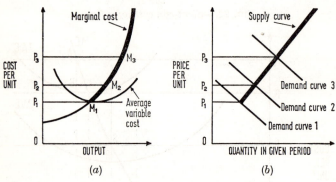

FIG. 24.—*Supply in the short period*

Fig. 24 shows:

  (a) The supply curve of a single firm.
  (b) The supply and demand curves for the industry.

Demand curve 1 gives a price of P_1 (Fig. 24(b)); the firm will produce P_1M_1. Demand curve 2 gives a price of P_2; the firm will produce P_2M_2 (Fig. 24(a)).

3. The long-run average cost curve. For each scale of operations there is a short-run average cost curve. As the scale of operations, associated with larger plant, gets bigger the short-run average cost curve will have a lower minimum average cost (*see* **1** above). After an optimum size has been reached—the size that gives the lowest average cost per unit of output (*OM* in Fig. 25)—the short-run average cost curves begin to have a higher minimum cost per unit of output due to diseconomies of management (*see* **1** above). This is shown in Fig. 25. The long-run average cost curve is tangential to the set of short-run average cost curves.

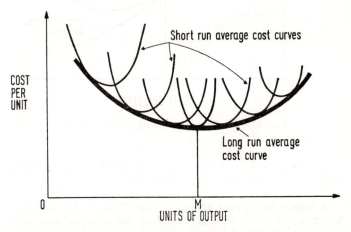

FIG. 25.—*Long-run average cost curve*

Long-run average cost is the average cost per unit of output when the entrepreneur has had time to vary all the factors of production so that he has the most profitable-size plant and the best proportion of fixed and variable factors for any given output.

When a firm has not reached its optimum size, it will pay a firm to under-use a larger plant, rather than to use fully a smaller one, even though this would give the lowest short-run average costs. This is shown in Fig. 26.

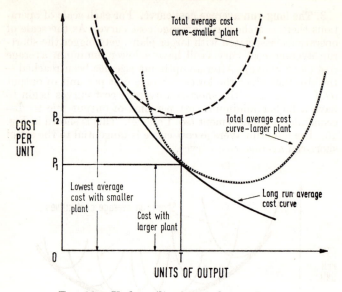

FIG. 26.—*Under-utilisation of plant and costs*

At output OT, cost per unit with smaller plant is OP_2. With bigger plant, not fully utilised, the cost is OP_1.

4. Supply in the long period. Figure 25 shows the long-run average cost curve of a firm. A *long-run marginal cost curve* can be obtained from this average cost curve and this is shown in Fig. 27. *Long-run marginal cost is the cost of an additional unit of output when all the factors of production are variable.*

NOTE

(i) Long-run marginal costs (on diagram designated LMC) may be less or greater than short-run marginal costs (designated $SRMC_1$, $SRMC_2$ and $SRMC_3$). Long-run marginal costs depend upon the costs of *all* the factors of production; short-run marginal costs depend solely on the costs of the *variable* factors. Whether long-run marginal costs are less than or greater than short-run marginal costs depends upon the output the short-run plant is producing.

(ii) Short-run and long-run marginal costs are equal where short-run and long-run average cost curves are tangential. This is shown in Fig. 27 for output OT, OM and OZ.

(iii) At output OM (the output of long-run lowest average cost), long-run average cost equals long-run marginal cost. This point is also the lowest average cost of short-run average cost curve 2. OM is the optimum size of the firm.

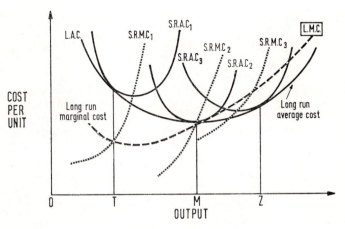

FIG. 27.—*Supply in the long period*

The long-run supply curve of a firm is its long-run marginal cost curve. If prices at any given time were higher than the marginal cost due to increased demand, an economic rent would emerge. New firms would enter the industry and the additional supply lower prices until they coincided with the marginal cost. The supply curve of the industry is the sum of the individual supply curves.

PROGRESS TEST 5

1. Contrast the short-run supply curve of a firm with the long-run supply curve. **(2, 4)**

2. What do you understand by indivisibilities and what is their effect upon cost? **(1)**

3. How is the long-run average cost curve derived? **(3)**

4. What is the relationship between the supply curve of a firm and the supply curve of the industry? **(2)**

5. When is it profitable (*a*) to have a larger installation and not fully work it, (*b*) to have a smaller plant and over-utilise it? **(3)**

6. How is a firm's output determined in the short-run? **(2)**

7. Are there any limits to the economies of specialisation? **(1)**

8. What is the relationship between short-run and long-run marginal costs? **(4)**

CHAPTER VI

PRICE DETERMINATION

1. Competition of the many. Firms may sell the same commodity or commodities which although different in some respect yet nevertheless are sufficiently good substitutes (their cross elasticities are high) for there to be real competition among them. If the commodity is *exactly* the same, it is known as a *homogeneous product*; if not, as a *differentiated product*.

> "*Differentiation* may be based on certain characteristics of the product itself such as exclusive patented features; trade marks; trade-names; peculiarities of the package or container; or singularity in quality, design, colour or style. It may also exist with respect to the conditions surrounding its sale. In the retail trade, to take only one instance, these conditions include such things as the convenience of the seller's location, the general tone and character of his establishment, his way of doing business, his reputation for fair dealing, courtesy, efficiency and all the personal links which attach his customers either to himself or to those employed by him. In so far as these and other intangible factors vary from seller to seller, the 'product' in each case is different, for customers take them into account more or less and may be regarded as purchasing them along with the commodity itself." (Chamberlin. *The Theory of Monopolistic Competition*. Harvard University Press.)
>
> "It is frequently implied that product differentiation is exclusively monopolistic in nature, but this is surely wrong. Under perfect competition there would still be many qualities of goods of certain types because of the great variety of tastes and needs of consumers. . . . It is therefore necessary to eliminate differences in prices due to differences in costs for these price differentials *would* also exist under competition. Frequently this correction will reduce greatly the discrepancies to be explained in terms of monopolistic powers." (Stigler. *The Theory of Price*. Macmillan Company, N.Y.)

There are *many* firms if the *variations in output* of any single one alone are so small in relation to the total output of the whole industry that they have *negligible effect* on the total supply and hence *upon the price*.

Figure 28 shows the cost curves of a single firm, one of many all selling a homogeneous product. The firm is a *price-taker*, the price being *OP*. The quantity the firm sells has no effect on the price, hence average revenue (price) is the same as marginal revenue. The output of the firm will be *OM* (the

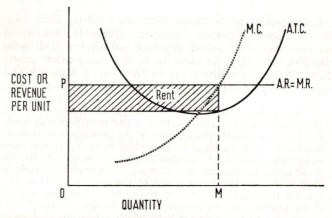

FIG. 28.—*Homogeneous product; fixed number of firms*

output that equates marginal revenue and marginal cost). At this output the cost is *OC* per unit. There is an economic rent of *CP* per unit of output. The total rent is indicated in the diagram by the shaded portion. If there is a fixed number of firms and no other firms enter the industry this firm will continue to receive this economic rent.

If there is complete freedom of entry other firms will enter the industry; the increase in supply will cause the price to fall until the economic rent disappears. The position of the firm will then be as in Fig. 29. At output *OM*, Marginal revenue = Marginal cost = Average revenue = Average cost. This is perfect competition.

When the *product is differentiated* each firm has, in effect, a monopoly of its own product. Not a very powerful monopoly, however, because its products have very good substitutes in the form of the products of its competitors—the cross-elasticity is high. Nevertheless, it is a *price-maker*. Its sales will depend

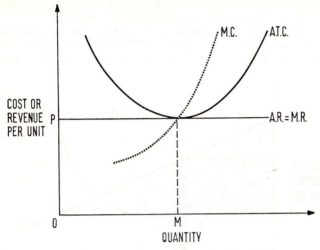

Fig. 29.—*Homogeneous product; freedom of entry*

upon the price it charges. It does not have to charge the same price as its competitors, for it is selling a different product. It is a different product if the customers think it is (perhaps, as the result of advertising and a brand name).

The output of the firm increases as the price falls; the average revenue curve is a sloping one. Since the average revenue curve slopes downwards, the marginal revenue curve is below it. This is illustrated as follows:

Average Revenue (Price) shillings	Output units	Total Revenue shillings	Marginal Revenue shillings
6	4,000	24,000	—
5	5,000	25,000	$\frac{1,000}{1,000} = 1 \cdot 00$
4	9,000	36,000	$\frac{11,000}{4,000} = 2 \cdot 75$
3	10,000	30,000	$-\frac{6,000}{1,000} = -6 \cdot 00$

NOTE: Although the marginal revenue sometimes falls, and sometimes rises, it is *always* below the average revenue.

Figure 30 shows the cost curves and the revenue curves of a firm, one of many, selling a differentiated product.

The output of the firm is OM (equating marginal cost and marginal revenue). The price is OP, but the cost is only OC. Economic rent is CP per unit. Rent, shown by the shaded

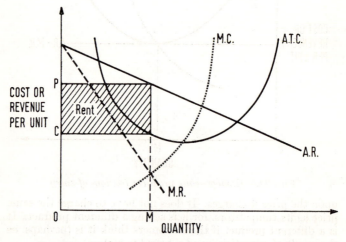

Fig. 30.—*Differentiated product; fixed number of firms*

portion of the diagram, will be received by the firm until other firms, attracted by the abnormal profits, enter the industry.

NOTE

(i) Excess capacity.
(ii) Product not produced at lowest average costs.

When other firms enter the industry, although they are producing differentiated products, it does mean that the demand for the first firm's products will be less at each price. The average revenue curve will shift towards the left. With free entry, firms will continue to enter the industry until the abnormal profits disappear. This is shown in Fig. 31.

The firm whose cost and revenue curves are shown in this diagram will produce OM, this being the output that equates marginal cost and marginal revenue. This output will be sold

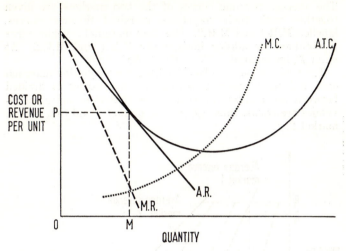

COST OR
REVENUE   P
PER UNIT

FIG. 31.—*Differentiated product; freedom of entry*

for OP per unit. The cost per unit is also OP. No abnormal profit is earned.

NOTE: Where many firms sell differentiated products which are in competition, this is known as *monopolistic competition*. Where no abnormal profits are earned, there is excess capacity and the cost of production is higher than the lowest average costs.

2. Price discrimination. When it is possible for markets to be kept distinct, it is usually possible to charge different prices in the different markets.

CONDITIONS FOR DISCRIMINATION TO BE POSSIBLE AND PROFIT-ABLE

(1) Monopoly or collusion among sellers.

(2) Total demand able to be divided into markets with different elasticities of demand.

(3) Cost of separating markets small in relation to differences in elasticities.

Figure 32 illustrates the case of two independent markets.

The average revenue curves of the two markets are given together with their respective marginal revenue curves, labelled M.R.1 and M.R.2. The total marginal revenue curve is obtained by adding horizontally M.R.1 and M.R.2. At point E, for example, $RE = RL + RM$.

The total output will be OT (this output equating marginal cost and total marginal revenue). This output is divided between the markets in such a way that their marginal revenues are equal; thus OQ_1 goes to market 1 and OQ_2 goes to market 2.

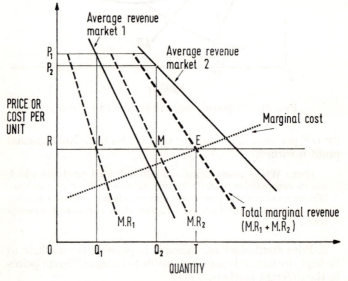

Fig. 32.—*Price discrimination*

The price for market 1 will be OP_1 and the price for market 2 will be OP_2. The higher price is the result of a more inelastic demand.

NOTE

(i) The prices cannot differ by more than the cost of moving the commodity from one market to the other.

(ii) Discrimination involves costs and even if demand elasticities in the markets are equal discrimination may still arise if marginal costs in the markets differ.

3. Monopoly and monopsony.

A *monopoly* is defined by Stigler as *a firm producing a commodity for which there are no close substitutes.* The analysis required to determine the output and price for such a firm is the same as is shown in Fig. 30.

A *monopsony* exists where there is *a single buyer who is able to impose a price.*

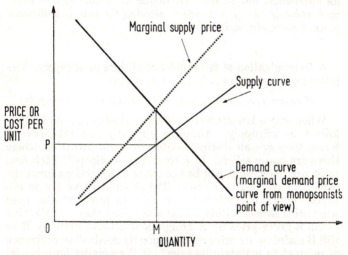

Fig. 33.—*Monopsony*

In Fig. 33 is shown the marginal demand curve of a monopsonist—the amount he is willing to pay for successive units—and the marginal supply curve—the amount it will cost him for successive units. He will purchase *OM*, this being the quantity that equates marginal supply price and marginal demand price. It will cost him *OP* per unit, that being the supply price for that quantity.

NOTE: Since the supply curve slopes upwards, the marginal supply curve is above the supply curve.

The monopsony demand curve. Refer to Fig. 12 in Chapter II. Each point of tangency between the price lines and the indifference curves indicates the marginal rate of substitution between money and commodity X, that is it indicates the sum of money—the *marginal demand price*—that will be paid for a further unit of X. Each marginal demand price depends upon the amount of X already possessed. It is this concept that distinguishes the marginal demand curve (plotted in the same way as the normal demand curve) from the conventional demand curve. On the *conventional demand curve each point is an alternative*, but in the case of the *marginal demand curve each point is one of a sequence, showing the marginal demand price of successive units.*

4. Determination of price under conditions of oligopoly. The following question was set in a final paper:

How are prices determined under conditions of oligopoly?

When only a few firms comprise an industry the condition is known as oligopoly. Although oligopoly can take several forms they are all distinguishable from the situation where there are many sellers. In a condition of oligopoly each firm must ask itself what will be the effect of its actions upon the behaviour of the other firms. The demand curve for an oligopolistic firm depends not only upon the price but also upon what other firms are doing, what sales policy they are following —will a lower price by A bring about a lower price by B or will B maintain its price relying upon its goodwill or difference of product to maintain its sales? If B reacts by lowering its price will A then lower its price again and so on? There are as many solutions to price determination in oligopoly as there are different assumptions one cares to make; and for many assumptions, especially those that approximate to reality, the price will be indeterminate.

There are two main types of oligopoly; perfect oligopoly, where there is no differentiation of product so that a cut in the price of one firm must immediately result in an identical cut by all the other firms and imperfect oligopoly where the product is differentiated enough so that a price cut on the part of one firm does not immediately result in a retaliatory price cut on the part of the others.

Perfect oligopoly

A firm's sales curve under conditions of perfect oligopoly, unlike one under conditions of perfect competition, will not be perfectly elastic, because a change in the price of one firm is followed by a change in the prices of the others. Thus, its sales do not expand indefinitely or fall to zero as would be the case under perfect competition. If the price of A is lowered, then the price of B and C will also be lowered to maintain their sales. At these lower prices, the total sales will increase and the absolute share of each firm will increase. Similarly, a rise in price by firm A would be followed by a rise in price of his competitors in order that they too could take advantage of the profit-making opportunities that induced A to raise his price. We should expect firms to be quicker in lowering prices (to maintain sales) than in raising them. The sales curve would therefore be more elastic above the current price than below. This is the "kinked" demand curve. But now suppose the oligopolist A changes his price. A new demand curve would have to be drawn "kinked" about the new price.

The firm's equilibrium position will depend upon the assumptions made about the way producers react to each other's behaviour. They may act in collusion and behave as a single monopolist. The result of this may be that the total output and price is such that the aggregate profit is a maximum. The price would then be above the average cost in each firm. On the other hand, they may undercut each other until the price falls to the lowest possible point consistent with the survival of the firms, in which case the price would be equal to average cost. They might compete by introducing differentiation of product (by means of a brand name and advertising), adding services, giving favourable terms of payment rather than by price-cutting. The price is therefore indeterminate. Everything depends upon the endless assumptions one makes concerning the extent of the degree of co-operation or competition between the producers. All that can be said is that the price will be between a monopoly price and a perfect competition price.

Imperfect oligopoly

Where the product is sufficiently differentiated and price cuts by one firm do not automatically bring about price cuts

C

by the others, price cutting will be common. Firms may often formulate policies upon the assumption that other firms will not retaliate. An unstable situation arises. Firm A cuts prices because its marginal revenue is greater than its marginal cost. This is justified provided that B does not also cut prices. B, we will suppose, does not react immediately—his product is sufficiently differentiated. Later, however, he may find it profitable to cut his price to an even greater extent than A, to whom he is losing trade. B's low price may now bring a still further cut from A and so on.

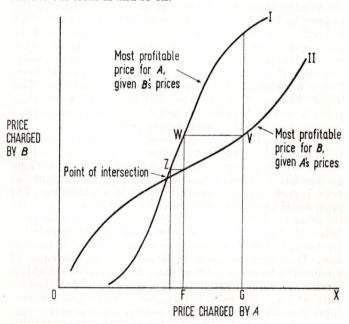

FIG. 34.—*Price determination under imperfect oligopoly*

In Fig. 34, if, from the point U on curve I a perpendicular is dropped on to OX, then OG is the most profitable price A can charge for B's price of UG. However, if A charges OG it will pay B to charge VG, shown by curve II. If B now charges VG, which is the same as WF, it can be seen from curve I that A's most profitable price is OF. If price cutting continues, the point Z will ultimately be reached when it pays neither firm to cut its prices. Whether this is a stable position or not depends on whether both firms are making at least normal profits. If not, one will go out of business, leaving a monopoly. They may perhaps come to an agreement to raise prices, that is, again act as a monopoly. They make further efforts to increase the differentiation of their products still further. If, on the other hand, at the point of equilibrium they are both making abnormal profits, other firms may enter the industry and disturb the equilibrium prices.

NOTE: This answer is given in essay form. Generally speaking this is the form required in Economics exams and not a series of notes marked (*a*), (*b*), (*c*). A very limited amount of under-lining is sometimes useful where, for example, italics would be used in print.

5. The "kinked" demand curve. Oligopolists often consider their average revenue curve to be "kinked" around the current price. This is illustrated in Fig. 35.

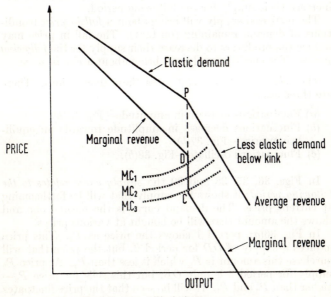

FIG. 35.—*The "kinked" demand curve*

If the price is lowered, other firms will follow and this is true whether it is a question of perfect or imperfect oligopoly. The lower price induces greater sales and each oligopolist will probably have some share in these increased sales.

If, on the other hand, price is increased above P, the oligopolist will rapidly lose trade to his competitors.

It follows from these considerations that the demand curve above P is more elastic than the demand curve below P. The marginal revenue curve will therefore be discontinuous (shown in the diagram by the line DC).

The price is fixed at the point where marginal cost and marginal revenue are equal. It can be seen from the diagram that marginal cost can vary (three marginal cost curves are shown) without altering the price. *Prices can be stable although costs alter.*

6. The cobweb theorem. A favourable price for certain commodities (for example, farm produce) may induce producers, in the expectation that this price will be maintained, to increase their supply for the following period.

The increased supply will bring about a *fall in price* (conditions of demand remaining constant). The fall in price may induce the producers to decrease their supply for the *following period*. The smaller supply will bring about a *rise in price*.

The *cobweb theorem* investigates these fluctuations. There are three cases:

    (a) Fluctuations increase in amplitude—Fig. 36(b).
    (b) Fluctuations decrease in amplitude towards an equilibrium price—Fig. 37(b).
    (c) Fluctuations oscillate—Fig. 38(b).

In Figs. 36, 37, 38 and 39 the *supply curve relates to the following period*; it shows the supply that will be forthcoming at current price. The demand curve is the normal one and shows the amount that will be bought at various prices.

In Fig. 36(a), period 1 shows the price as P_1. This price induces a supply of OD for period 2, but the price that will purchase this amount is P_2 which is less than P_1. At price P_2 supply for period 3 is only OB, but this sells for price P_3—higher than P_2 and P_1. It will be seen that the price fluctuates by increasing amounts. This is illustrated in Fig. 36(b).

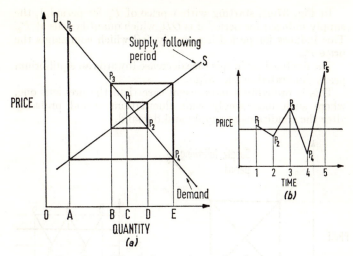

FIG. 36.—*Cobweb theorem-increasing fluctuations*

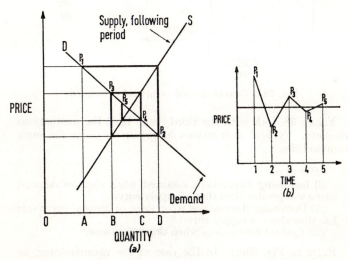

FIG. 37.—*Cobweb theorem—fluctuations towards equilibrium*

In Fig. 37(a), starting with a price of P_1 for period 1, the supply induced for period 2 is OD, which quantity sells at P_2. This induces for period 3 a supply OB which commands the price P_3.

The fluctuations in this case decrease towards an equilibrium price, illustrated in Fig. 37(b).

This is probably a more usual case than the previous one, where such increasingly wide fluctuations would probably alter the conditions of supply and demand.

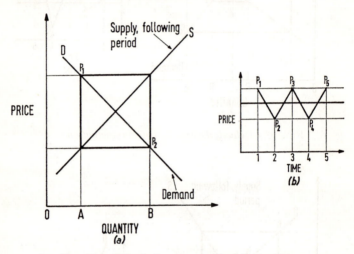

FIG. 38.—*Cobweb theorem—cyclical fluctuations*

Figure 38 deals with the third case. Here the fluctuations oscillate. Cyclical fluctuations in prices do occur for some commodities.

NOTE

(i) Increasing fluctuations occurred when slope of demand curve was greater than that of supply curve.

(ii) Decreasing fluctuations when slope of demand curve was less than slope of supply curve.

(iii) Cyclical fluctuations when slopes the same.

Refer to Fig. 39(a). In the case of the manufacturer, as contrasted with the farmer, he can usually increase output by

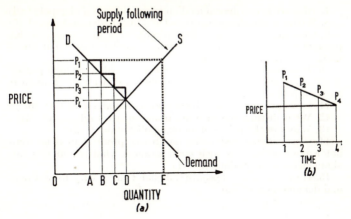

Fig. 39.—*Cobweb theorem—small adjustments*

small amounts fairly quickly. If the price is, say P_1, instead of producing a quantity OE for the next period, he will increase his output by, say AB, in a short period, which will have the effect of lowering the price to P_2. Again, he will increase his output in a further short period, say by BC; this will lower prices still further to P_3. He will thus proceed by short incremental adjustments towards equilibrium price—Fig. 39(*b*).

The cobweb theorem analysis is useful in showing that perfect competition, unlike monopoly, leads to unstable prices.

PROGRESS TEST 6

1. What makes two products different products and not two of the same product? (**1**)
2. XYZ Ltd. is one of a large number of firms all selling exactly the same product. Under what circumstances would this firm (*a*) earn rent, (*b*) not earn rent? (**1**)
3. Give examples of a price-taker and a price-maker. How do their average revenue curves differ? (**1**)
4. What is meant by monopolistic competition? (**1**)
5. When a product is sold in two independent markets, in which of them will the price be higher? (**2**)
6. What is (*a*) monopoly, (*b*) monopsony? (**3**)

7. How are prices determined under conditions of oligopoly? **(4)**

8. What are the characteristics of a "kinked" demand curve? **(5)**

9. How might a farmer react towards very high prices for his products? If all farmers reacted in a similar way, what effect might it have on prices? **(6)**

10. How might a manufacturer react towards very high prices? If all manufacturers reacted in the same way, what effect might it have on prices? **(6)**

11. In what way is the cobweb theorem analysis useful? **(6)**

12. What distinguishes perfect from imperfect oligopoly? **(4)**

13. Why are the prices of an oligopolist stable? **(5)**

14. Can a monopolist make no greater profit than if he were not a monopolist? In such circumstances what would you say about his cost of production? **(1)**

15. How does a monopsonist's demand curve vary from a normal demand curve? **(3)**

CHAPTER VII

LABOUR

1. Supply of labour. Figure 40 shows the indifference map of a certain individual, depicting various combinations of leisure and income. Leisure is measured along the y-axis and income along the x-axis. The total amount of leisure available is 16 hours per day (the other 8 hours not being considered available for exchanging for income since they are necessarily reserved for sleeping, eating, etc.).

Six indifference curves are shown, I_1, I_2, I_3, etc. Six price lines are also shown, $PL1$, $PL2$, $PL3$, etc. Their slopes indicate

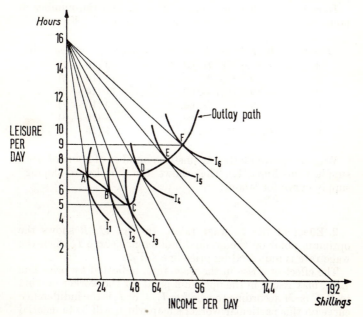

Fig. 40.—*Outlay path for income*

57

the wage rate, *e.g.* $PL1$ has a slope of $\dfrac{24 \text{ shillings}}{16 \text{ hours}} = 1s. 6d.$ per hour. $PL6$ indicates $\dfrac{192}{16} = 12s.$ per hour. The less the steepness of the slope the higher the wage rate (the less the price of income in terms of leisure).

The points of tangency of indifference curves and price lines such as A, B, C, etc., shown in the indifference map are the points most beneficial to the worker. At point B, for example, he would exchange 10 hours leisure (leaving him 6 hours) for 30s. (price line indicating 3s. per hour).

The outlay path, joining points A, B, C, D, E and F, shows that as the wage rate increases, from $PL1$ to $PL6$, the effect on the amount of work supplied (leisure exchanged for income), is sometimes to increase it and sometimes to decrease it as shown in schedule below.

Here is a schedule showing wage rates and the number of hours worked, taken from the indifference map of Fig. 40.

Point	Wage rates (per hour)	Number of hours of work
A	$PL1$ ($\frac{24}{16}$) 1s. 6d.	9 (16 − 7)
B	$PL2$ ($\frac{48}{16}$) 3s. 0d.	10 (16 − 6)
C	$PL3$ ($\frac{64}{16}$) 4s. 0d.	11 (16 − 5)
D	$PL4$ ($\frac{96}{16}$) 6s. 0d.	9 (16 − 7)
E	$PL5$ ($\frac{144}{16}$) 9s. 0d.	8 (16 − 8)
F	$PL6$ ($\frac{192}{16}$) 12s. 0d.	7 (16 − 9)

Wage rates are plotted against the number of hours of work supplied in Fig. 41. This shows the "backward-sloping" supply curve for labour.

2. Effect of rise in wage rates. In Fig. 42, R shows the optimum point on the original indifference curve I_0 when the wage rate is indicated by price line LW_1.

The effect of a rise in the wage rate, indicated by price line LW_2, may result in the optimum point for the worker moving to P, U or M according to whether I_1, I_2 or I_3 is the indifference curve on this particular worker's map which will be tangential to the new price line.

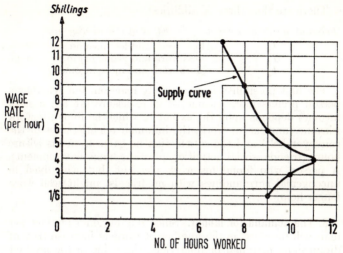

FIG. 41.—*Labour supply curve*

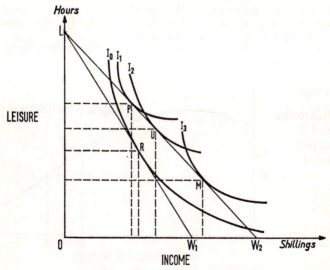

FIG. 42.—*Effect of rise in wage rates*

There are thus three possibilities:

Relevant indifference curve	*Effect of rise in wage rate*
I_1	Less work and less income
I_2	Less work and (same or) more income
I_3	More work and more income

The first possibility is an unlikely reaction, but whether a person prefers more income or more leisure (at the cost of income) depends upon the extent to which he finds his work irksome (unpleasant work, the inhuman relentlessness of the conveyor belt) and the satisfaction he gains from his leisure hours (friends, social activities, pleasant home environment). A person who found his work pleasant, but who lived in uncongenial surroundings with no friends, might well work longer hours.

3. The demand for labour. Since the marginal product per man will decrease as the number of workers increase (law of diminishing marginal productivity), the value of the product will decrease.

In Fig. 43, the discounted value of the marginal product is measured along the y-axis (discounted because wages are paid before the revenue from the product is obtained). Along the x-axis the number of workers is plotted.

If the wage is W_L, the demand will be for ON_2 workers: if the wage is W_H, the demand will be for ON_1 workers.

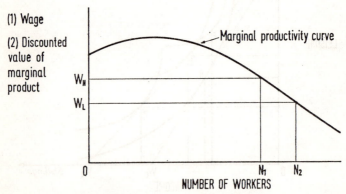

FIG. 43.—*Demand for labour*

4. The monopsonist buyer of labour. Often where there are no regulated wage rates, a firm is in a position of being a sole buyer of a certain type of labour.

Under such monopsonistic conditions, additional men can only be obtained by increasing the wage rate; the marginal cost of labour is therefore higher than the wage of the marginal worker (*see* Schedule 2).

In Fig. 44, a demand curve for labour is obtained by plotting the data from Schedule 1. The supply curve and the marginal cost curve are obtained from the data in Schedule 2.

SCHEDULE 1

Marginal productivity schedule

No. of workers	Discounted value of marginal product £
4	7
5	6
6	5
7	4
8	3
9	2

SCHEDULE 2

Labour Cost—Monopsony

No. of workers	Wage per worker	Total wages £	Marginal cost £
4	£1 10s.	6	–
5	£2	10	4
6	£2 10s.	15	5
7	£3	21	6
8	£3 10s.	28	7
9	£4	36	8

SCHEDULE 3

Labour Cost—Perfect Competition

No. of workers	Wage per worker £	Total wages £	Marginal costs £
4	3	12	–
5	3	15	3
6	3	18	3
7	3	21	3
8	3	24	3
9	3	27	3

It will be seen that this particular firm will employ six workers; this is the number that equates marginal cost and marginal productivity. To employ seven instead of six would add £6 to cost (*see* Schedule 2) but only £4 to revenue (*see* Schedule 1). Hence a seventh man would not be employed.

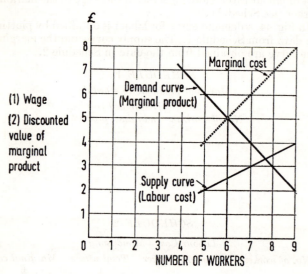

FIG. 44.—*The monopsonist buyer of labour*

The six men would be employed at a wage of £2 10s. Under conditions of perfect competition where the firm could buy as much labour as it wanted without its demand affecting the wage rate, eight men would have been employed at a wage of £3 (*see* Schedules 1 and 3).

5. The economy of high wages. Refer to Fig. 45. ON_2 workers will be employed at a wage OW_2. Should the wage be raised to OW_1 the number of workers employed will fall to ON_1. It is suggested that the higher wage may raise the standard of living to such an extent that the productivity of the workers will increase so that the demand curve shifts to the right and OW_1 becomes the equilibrium wage.

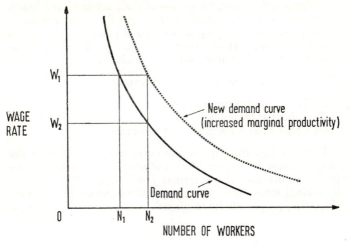

FIG. 45.—*Economy of high wages*

6. Trade unions and bargaining. The monopsonist power of the buyer of labour is destroyed by the creation of trade unions, and the position is then often one of bilateral monopoly. The trade union will have a figure below which it will not go, but asks for a higher one; the employers have a figure they will not exceed, but offer a lower one. The actual figure agreed upon will be somewhere between the union's lowest figure and the employer's highest; exactly where will depend upon their respective bargaining powers.

The bargaining powers of the workers and employers are unequal because:

(*a*) *Large numbers of workers face a few employers* who will often be in close contact with each other. There will be competition among the workers, but not among the employers. Trade unions can, to a great extent, overcome this disadvantage of the workers.

(*b*) *Labour is inseparable from the worker.* The worker, unlike the capitalist, cannot transfer his capital to other fields where it can earn him an income. Again, he cannot store his labour. A day without work means a permanent loss of income.

Trade unions can, by means of their accumulated funds, extend the workers' ability to hold out for a better wage.

(c) *The worker is propertyless.* He depends upon a flow of income to support himself and his family. He has little or no reserves and cannot therefore "wait."

The trade unions' power is limited because:

(a) The worker is propertyless.
(b) Labour is immobile.
(c) Labour has no control over resources.

Refer to Fig. 46. The supply curve is the addition of the supply curves of the individual workers and the demand curve is the addition of the marginal productivity curves of the individual firms. OW_1 is the equilibrium wage, and at that wage ON_1 people will be employed.

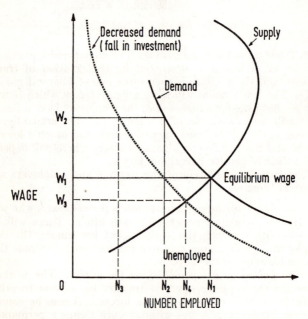

FIG. 46.—*Trade unions and bargaining power*

If now, the trade union succeeds in raising the wage rate to W_2, employment will fall to ON_2 and a number of people will be unemployed. After a time the supply of labour may well fall and the amount of unemployment be too small to exert any downward pressure on wages.

The trade union will tolerate the unemployment since, if investment in the industry increases, the unemployment will disappear, but if, in the first place, the trade union had accepted a lower wage rate, the increased investment would have necessitated the trade union fighting for the increased wage.

If, however, investment falls as indicated by the decreased demand curve, employment must fall to ON_3. The large number of unemployed would probably bring the wage down to round about OW_3, lower than the original equilibrium wage.

Since capitalists are more likely to cut down on investment rather than consumption when their income falls, it would appear that the bargaining power of trade unions is indeed weak. However, in an expanding economy, labour is able to get higher wages by reducing the rate of increase of consumption of capitalists, without affecting the growth of investment and hence labour productivity.

The bargaining power of labour is dependent not only on the labour market but also on the commodity markets of the employer. If the employer is a monopsonist in buying his raw materials and a monopolist in selling his product, he can offset higher wages by the lower cost of raw materials and higher prices to the consumer. However, such an increase of wages brings benefits to one group of people at the expense of other groups. Such action cannot, therefore, lead to a general improvement in wage rates.

7. Labour and technical progress. The result of technical advances is that the product or service will be produced at a lower cost.

Technical advances may take the form of:

(a) *Labour-saving inventions.* Capital will be substituted for labour. The saving in labour costs will be greater than the cost of additional capital. Examples: machine tools, automated processes.

(b) *Capital-saving inventions.* Labour will be substituted for capital, or there will be less capital without an increase in labour. The saving in capital costs will be greater than the additional cost of labour (if any). Examples: radio communications, air transport.

Any big invention will generally lead to some temporary unemployment caused by the readjustment made necessary by its introduction. But, it should be noted that in an *expanding industry*, the introduction of a new invention may be the alternative to increasing the labour force (which may not be possible). In this case, even readjustment unemployment may be avoided.

The long-term effect on employment. This can be demonstrated by the following two examples.

(a) Any initial unemployment caused by the introduction of the invention will quickly become offset by increased employment in the same or other industries. The introduction of the invention will have the effect of lowering the cost of the product or service.

This will lead to the lowering of the price and an extension of the demand, which if elastic, may be considerable. This extension of demand will re-absorb unemployed workers in their own industry. In addition, labour will be required to produce the capital goods.

(b) Where there is low substitutability between capital and labour, unemployment must follow the introduction of real capital. A labour-saving invention will lead to a great amount of capital being used by each worker. There will, however, be no real capital available for the workers who have become unemployed as the result of the introduction of the invention.

The length of unemployment will depend upon how quickly the economy adds to its capital equipment.

PROGRESS TEST 7

1. Why does the supply curve for labour slope backwards? **(1, 2)**
2. What is the effect of a rise in wage rates upon the amount of work done? **(2)**
3. What determines the demand for labour? **(3)**

4. What is the effect of a trade union having successfully negotiated a wage rate higher than the equilibrium rate? **(5, 6)**

5. Where a firm is a monopsonist in respect of its employment of labour, how will (*a*) the wage rate, (*b*) the number of workers employed, differ from where the firm has to compete with other firms for its labour force? **(4)**

6. Summarise the bargaining powers of a trade union. **(6)**

7. What is (*a*) the short-term effect, (*b*) the long-term effect, upon employment of the introduction of new inventions? **(7)**

8. It pays a firm to pay high wages. Discuss. **(5)**

9. What is meant by (*a*) a labour-saving invention, (*b*) a capital-saving invention? What is the effect on (*a*) the costs of production, (*b*) employment, when such inventions are introduced? **(7)**

10. What are the limitations to the bargaining powers of labour? **(6)**

CHAPTER VIII

CAPITAL

1. The marginal efficiency of investment. If an addition is
made to real capital (investment), it is expected to earn an
income. Let this income be I, earned in n years time. If the
cost of this investment (additional capital) is C, then:

$$C = \frac{I}{(1 + e)^n}$$

where e is *the marginal efficiency of investment*, that is the yield
or rate of interest earned on an investment of C.

In actuality, there will be a number of incomes for a number
of years, and

$$C = \frac{I_1}{1 + e} + \frac{I_2}{(1 + e)^2} + \frac{I_3}{(1 + e)^3} + \cdots \frac{I_n}{(1 + e)^n}$$

where $I_1, I_2, \ldots I_n$ are the incomes earned in successive years
for n years from an investment of C. Then e is the rate of
interest which equates all these future earnings with present
cost.

If e, the marginal efficiency of capital, is greater than the
current rate of interest, it will pay a firm to invest, since the
yield will be greater than the cost of borrowing money to make
the investment.

As the amount of investment increases, the marginal product will decrease (Law of diminishing marginal productivity).
Hence, as the amount of investment increases, the marginal
income will fall; the yield or marginal efficiency of investment
will fall.

*The greater the investment, the lower the marginal efficiency of
investment.*

In Fig. 47, MEI_1 is a marginal efficiency of investment curve.
Point M shows that the marginal efficiency of investment ON_0
is $E\%$; that is an investment of ON_0 would earn an income at
the rate of $E\%$. Similarly, point P indicates that an investment

of ON_1 (bigger than ON_0) would earn $R_1\%$; that is, the marginal efficiency of this larger investment ($R_1\%$) is less than the marginal efficiency ($E\%$) of the smaller investment. Point Q would indicate that an investment of ON_2 would earn $R_2\%$. If the current rate of interest is R_1 it will pay the firm to make an investment of ON_1.

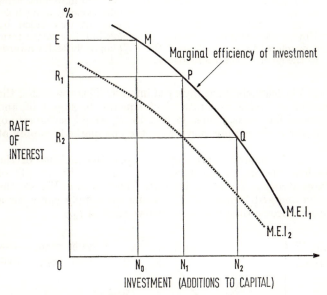

Fig. 47.—*The marginal efficiency of investment*

The MEI_1 curve is for a given stock of capital. If the stock of capital were greater, the marginal efficiency curve would be lower, say MEI_2. The current rate of interest would have to be R_2 for the firm to make the same investment of ON_1. *The MEI curve is a demand curve for investment.*

NOTE: The above analysis would seem to indicate that the rate of interest determines a firm's demand for investment. But evidence suggests that, in reality, firms pay little or no attention to interest rates when making investment decisions.

Labour-saving inventions will push the MEI curve upwards, since they increase the demand for capital; capital-saving inventions, on the other hand, push the *MEI* curve downwards.

The continual accumulation of capital also exerts a continual downwards pressure on the *MEI* curve.

NOTE

(i) The addition of all the *MEI* schedules of individual firms will give the demand for investment for the economy as a whole.

(ii) The marginal efficiency of investment was called by Keynes *the marginal efficiency of capital*, but this latter term now refers to the rate at which the *MEI* curve shifts downwards as the stock of capital increases.

2. The loanable funds theory of interest. This states that the rate of interest is that rate which equates the supply of, and demand for, loans. Thus, in Fig. 48, R_4 would be the rate of interest if the supply curve were the one marked "supply at I_1."

But the supply curve depends upon the incomes of the lenders; the higher the incomes, the greater the supply of loans at any given rate of interest. This is seen in Fig. 48, the curve marked "supply at I_4," being the supply curve for a higher income than the supply curve marked I_3.

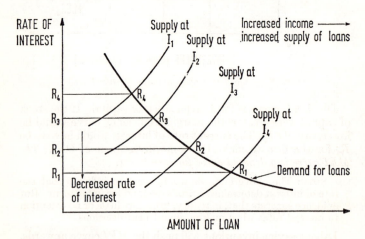

FIG. 48.—*Interest: loanable funds theory*

It will be further seen from the diagram that *as the income increases, the rate of interest falls.* It would be possible to draw up a schedule as follows:

Rate of interest to equate supply of, and demand for, loanable funds	*Income*
R_4	I_1
R_3	I_2
R_2	I_3
R_1	I_4

The rate of interest can be plotted against income—the *IS* curves of Figs. 50 and 51.

3. Keynesian theory of interest. This states that the rate of interest is that rate which equates the demand to hold money and the stock of money. Thus, in Fig. 49, R_1 is the rate of interest if the demand curve to hold money is the one marked I_1.

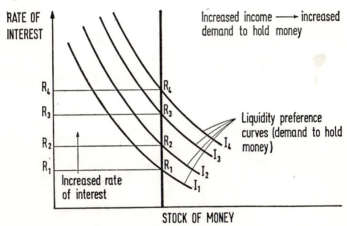

FIG. 49.—*Interest: Keynesian theory*

The demand to hold money, however, depends upon income; the higher the income, the greater the amount of money people wish to hold. This is illustrated in Fig. 49. I_4 is a demand curve for a higher income than I_3. I_3 is a demand curve for a higher income than I_2.

It will be seen that *as income rises, rate of interest rises.* It would be possible to draw up a schedule as follows:

Rate of interest to equate demand to hold money and stock of money	*Income*
R_4	I_4
R_3	I_3
R_2	I_2
R_1	I_1

The rates of interest can be plotted against income—the *LM* curves of Figs. 50 and 51.

4. The determination of interest. Both the loanable funds theory and the Keynesian theory of interest were inadequate explanations of how the rate of interest is determined. They both ignored the effect of income. An acceptable theory must take this into account.

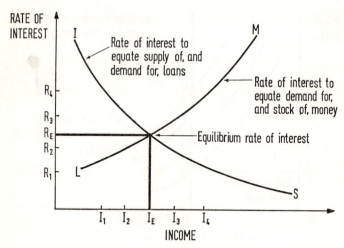

FIG. 50.—*Determination of interest*

In Fig. 50, the "*IS*" curve gives the rate of interest that will equate the supply of, and demand for, loanable funds at various levels of income (*see* 2 above). The "*LM*" curve gives the rate of interest that equates the stock of money and the demand to hold money at various levels of income (*see* **3** above). Where the two curves intersect, the *rate of interest* is one which: *Equates supply of, and demand for, loans,* AND *equates demand to hold money and stock of money at a determinable income.* (In Fig. 50, this rate will be R_E and the income will be I_E.)

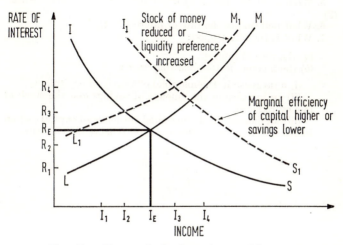

Fig. 51.—*Changes in the determinants of interest*

In Fig. 51, *IS* and *LM* are the curves relevant for the initial situation. The rate of interest will be R_E and the income I_E. Now consider a few possibilities:

(*a*) An increase in the marginal efficiency of capital or a decrease in the amount of savings moves *IS* to I_1S_1. Interest would rise to R_3 and income to I_4.

(*b*) *IS* curve remains unchanged, but stock of money is reduced or liquidity preference increased (there is a greater demand to hold money). *LM* moves to L_1M_1. Interest rises to R_3, but income falls to I_2.

(*c*) Both curves change, *LM* to L_1M_1 and *IS* to I_1S_1. Interest rises to R_4 and income to I_3.

PROGRESS TEST 8

1. What is meant by the marginal efficiency of investment? **(1)**

2. What will cause the *MEI* curve to move downwards? **(1)**

3. What is the effect of introducing inventions into industry upon the marginal efficiency of investment? **(1)**

4. What is the loanable funds theory of interest? What is its defect? **(2)**

5. What is the Keynesian theory of interest? What is its defect? **(3)**

6. What determines the rate of interest? **(4)**

7. What is the effect upon:

(*a*) the rate of interest,

(*b*) the income, in the following cases:

(i) a decrease in the marginal efficiency of capital,

(ii) an increase in the amount of savings *and* the stock of money reduced,

(iii) an increase in the marginal efficiency of capital *and* an increase in liquidity preference? **(4)** (Diagrams will help.)

CHAPTER IX

THE NATIONAL INCOME AND THE NATIONAL PRODUCT

1. The principles of national income accounting. These are:

(*a*) Incomes in return for work and the use of property *are* costs to firms. The total of such incomes *equals* the total costs to firms (factor costs). *Gross national income* equals *gross national product*.

(*b*) Incomes to people which are not factor costs are in the nature of transfer payments and are *not* part of the national income. They are redistributions of income.

Taxation which is an income of the government who collects it from people and spends it on their behalf is in this category. It is not part of the national income.

(*c*) The gross national product consists of goods and services which are consumed *and* those which are an addition to assets and are called investment. The gross national expenditure consists of expenditure on consumption goods and services *and* investment. Gross national expenditure therefore *equals* gross national product.

(*d*) The total goods and services produced in the United Kingdom is the gross domestic product. Part of this belongs to non-residents who obtain incomes from property in this country. On the other hand, residents of the United Kingdom possess part of other countries' domestic products. The difference between income payable abroad and income receivable from abroad is added or subtracted according to which is greater to the gross domestic product to give the gross national product.

(*e*) The term gross is used because in producing the goods and services capital (*e.g.* plant and machinery) is used up. This capital consumption (known by accountants as depreciation) when deducted from the gross national income gives *national income*.

2. Entries in the national income and expenditure accounts.

The national income and expenditure, its various concepts, and its composition will be presented in a number of different ways:

(*a*) in the form of double entry *social accounts*;
(*b*) as a *matrix*;
(*c*) as a *statement*;
(*d*) in the form of a series of *bar charts*; and
(*e*) as a *flow chart*.

In all these forms of presentation each entry will be numbered. The numbers of the entries and notes thereon follow:

(1) *Income from work.* This includes wages and salaries, income from self-employment (including farmers). It includes employer's contributions to national insurance which are considered as part of employee's income deducted at source.

(2) *Income from property-rent, interest and dividends.* This includes income from property abroad.

(3) *Transfer payments.* These include national insurance benefits, national assistance, family allowances, scholarships and maintenance allowances.

(4) *Expenditure on consumption goods by persons.* This includes consumers' expenditure abroad less expenditure by foreign tourists in the United Kingdom.

(5) *Taxes from persons.* This includes both employer's (*see* (1) above) and employee's national insurance contributions.

(6) *Savings by persons.* By definition the balance of income after spending on consumption goods and paying taxes.

(7) *Expenditure on consumption goods by government.* Of the £3365 million spent by central government, military defence accounted for £1871 million, the national health service £866 million, finance and tax collection £120 million and research £94 million. Of the £1742 million spent by local authorities, education accounted for £879 million, police £160 million, roads £140 million and sewerage and refuse disposal £108 million.

(8) *Gross domestic capital formation.* This consists of expenditure on fixed assets (buildings, vehicles, plant and machinery), either for replacing, or adding to, stock of existing fixed assets.

(9) *Imports and income paid abroad.* This includes not only imports of goods but also services (invisible imports). It also includes rents, interest, profits and dividends paid overseas amounting to £1002 million.

(10) *Exports and income received from abroad.* Included in this item is £1379 million for rent, interest, profits and dividends received from overseas by United Kingdom residents.

Net income from abroad £1379 million *less* £1002 million (*see* item (9) = £377 million).

(11) *Expenditure taxes (less subsidies).* *Expenditure taxes* (customs and excise duties, purchase tax, licences, stamp duties) are *added to factor costs* to give *market prices* whereas income taxes are a redistribution of incomes—incomes taken from the taxpayer and transferred to the government who spends them on behalf of the people as a whole.

Factor costs of £100 give rise to incomes of £100. An *income tax* of £20 means that the income receivers have only £80 to spend and the government spends the other £20. Together they can purchase the product of £100.

Factor costs of £100 give rise to incomes of £100. An *expenditure tax* of £20 means that the market price of the product is £120; the income receivers spend £100 and the government £20. Together they purchase £120 of product at market prices (the factor cost of this product being £100).

Subsidies are made to a producer or trader with the object of making his selling price less than the factor cost of production. They are negative expenditure taxes and are deducted from factor costs to give market prices.

NOTE: Rates are local taxes. They are treated as expenditure taxes in the National Income and Expenditure Blue Book. They add to the cost of housing.

(12) *Government grants paid abroad.* This consists of grants to colonial governments, financial assistance to overseas governments, subscriptions and contributions to international organisations, and war pensions and national insurance benefits paid to persons abroad.

(13) *Investment abroad.* This represents the net change in the value of overseas assets of United Kingdom residents. It is the sum of the net increase in overseas investments in real assets *plus* increase in net lending to overseas residents *plus* increases in gold and dollar reserves and official holdings of foreign currencies *less* increases in net liabilities in sterling and other currencies.

(14) *Rent, interest and dividends received by government.* The largest part of the central government income from this source is interest on loans to local authorities and public corporations.

(15) *National Debt interest and interest on local government debt.* These are in the nature of *transfer payments* and are included in items (2) and (14).

(16) *Profit from government trading.* This includes the surpluses of the trading departments of central government (except the Post Office which is now treated as a public corporation) and trading surpluses of local authorities engaged in providing water, transport, harbours, docks, etc.

(17) *Taxes on undistributed profits.* The taxes on distributed profits are deducted from dividends and paid to the Inland Revenue on behalf of the shareholders. Such taxation is included in (5) and is a redistribution of income; it is not a factor cost. The taxes on undistributed profits are a part of the profit which, although belonging to shareholders, is in the hands of the companies. It is a factor cost.

(18) *Undistributed profits.* This item includes the surpluses of the nationalised industries and the Post Office.

(19) *Savings by government.* Income *less* expenditure on consumption goods and services.

(20) *Grants paid abroad by persons.* Transfers abroad by persons including legacies and funds taken abroad by emigrants.

3. Social accounts.

Below are given the social accounts for the United Kingdom for the year 1963.

Persons

Receipts	£m.	Payments	£m.
(1) Income from work	20,292	(4) Expenditure on consumption goods	19,663
(2) Income from property (rent, interest and dividends)	2,807	(5) Taxation (including national insurance contributions)	3,810
(3) Transfer payments (national insurance benefits and other grants from public authorities)	2,230	(6) Savings	1,842
		(20) Grants abroad	14
	25,329		25,329

Firms

Output	£m.	Costs		£m.
(4) Consumption goods—persons	19,663	(1) Labour		20,292
(7) Consumption goods—government	5,107	Use of capital:		
(8) Gross domestic capital formation	4,968	(2) Rent, interest and dividends—persons	2,807	
		(14) Rent, interest and dividends—government	1,084	
Total domestic expenditure at market prices	29,738		3,891	
(10) Exports and income received from abroad 7,184		*Less*		
Less		(15) National Debt interest and local government debt interest	1,362	
(9) Imports and income paid abroad 6,921				2,529
		(16) Profit from government trading		74
Net investment abroad (plus grants paid abroad)	263	(17) Taxes on undistributed profits		878
		(18) Undistributed profits and surpluses of nationalised industries		2,763
Gross national product at market price	30,001			
Less				
(11) Taxes on expenditure (less subsidies)	3,465			
Gross national product at factor cost	26,536	*Gross national product at factor cost*		26,536

Abroad

	£m.		£m.
(9) Imports and income paid abroad	6,921	(10) Exports and income received	7,184
(12) Grants paid abroad:		from abroad	
government	136		
(20) Grants paid abroad:			
persons	14		
(13) Investment abroad *	113		
	7,184		7,184

* This agrees with the balance on current account of the Balance of Payments and represents the net change in value of overseas assets (both real and financial) of United Kingdom residents.

Government
central and local

	£m.		£m.
(5) Taxes from persons	3,810	(7) Consumption goods and services	5,107
(11) Expenditure taxes (less subsidies)	3,465	(3) Transfer payments	2,230
(14) Rent, interest and dividends	1,084	(15) National Debt interest and local	
(16) Profit from trading	74	government debt interest	1,362
(17) Taxes on undistributed profits	878	(19) Savings	476
		(12) Grants paid abroad	136
	9,311		9,311

In so far as the government is a productive unit, it is a "firm," and is included in the account headed "firms." The above account deals with government as a "collective" person receiving incomes and spending and saving on behalf of all the persons in a country.

Capital

	£m.		£m.
(6) Savings by persons	1,842	(8) Gross domestic capital formation	4,968
(19) Savings by government	476	(13) Net investment abroad	113
(18) Savings by firms	2,763		
	5,081		5,081

NOTE: Each item is *both* a receipt and a payment. It is instructive to trace the double entry in the above accounts. As each item is numbered this presents no difficulty.

Below is an extremely simplified version of the above social accounts.

Persons

	£m.		£m.
G.N.P. less (18) Incomes from work		(4) (7) (12) (20) Consumption goods	24,920
and property	23,773	(6) (19) Savings	2,318
(11) Expenditure taxes	3,465		
	27,238		27,238

Firms

	£m.		£m.
(4) (7) (12) (20) Consumption goods	24,920	G.N.P. less (18) Costs giving rise to	
(8) (13) Investment goods	5,081	incomes	23,773
		(18) Savings	2,763
		(11) Expenditure taxes	3,465
Gross national product at market price	30,001	Gross national product at market price	30,001

Capital

	£m.		£m.
(6) (8) (19) Savings	5,081	(8) (13) Investment	5,081

4. National income and expenditure.

Statement

	£m.	£m.
Personal income before taxation		
(1) Wages, salaries, etc.	20,292	
(2) Rent, interest and dividends	2,807	
(3) National insurance benefits, etc.	2,230	
		25,329
Add incomes *not received directly* by persons		
(18) Undistributed profits	2,763	
(17) Taxes on undistributed profits	878	
(14 & 16) Government income from trading and property	1,158	
	4,799	
Less		
(3 & 15) Transfer payments and debt interest included in above	3,592	
		1,207
GROSS NATIONAL PRODUCT AT FACTOR COST		26,536
Add		
(11) Expenditure taxes (less subsidies)		3,465
GROSS NATIONAL PRODUCT AT MARKET PRICES		30,001
(4 & 7) Consumption goods and services	24,770	
(8) Gross domestic capital formation	4,968	
TOTAL DOMESTIC EXPENDITURE AT MARKET PRICES		29,738
(13) Investment abroad	113	
(12 & 30) Grants abroad	150	
		263
GROSS NATIONAL EXPENDITURE		30,001
GROSS DOMESTIC PRODUCT AT FACTOR COST		26,159
Add Net income from abroad		377
GROSS NATIONAL PRODUCT AT FACTOR COST		26,536
Less Capital consumption*		2,324
NATIONAL INCOME		24,212

* This is an estimate of the capital resources used up in current production.

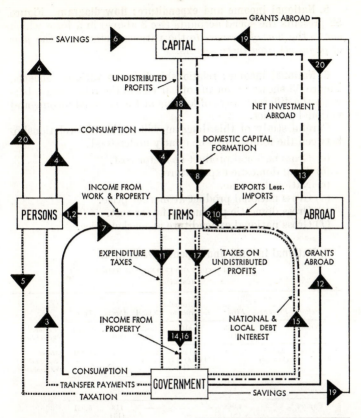

The arrows indicate direction of payment.

The numbers in the arrows refer to correspondingly numbered entries on the bar charts, the matrix, in the social accounts & the statement.

ITEM 18 both savings & factor cost
ITEM 17 both taxation & factor cost
ITEM 15 both transfer payment & deduction from factor costs

————————	Savings
— — — — —	Investment
—·—·—·—·—	Incomes & Factor costs
▬▬▬▬▬▬	Goods, Services & Grants
··················	Taxation & Transfer payments

Fig. 52.—*National income and expenditure: flow chart*

D

5. National income and expenditure: flow diagram. Figure 52 presents the social accounts (*see* **3** above) in a form which shows the *flow of incomes to* the various sectors and the *flow of payments from* these sectors.

6. National income: relationship between various concepts. Figure 53 shows by means of bar charts the relationship between the different ways of looking at the national income and national product.

Careful study of this diagram will enable the relationship between the following to be clearly understood:

(*a*) Gross national product at factor cost.
(*b*) Total domestic expenditure.
(*c*) National income.
(*d*) Gross national product at market price.
(*e*) Gross domestic product at factor cost.
(*f*) Gross national expenditure at market price.

7. National income and expenditure matrix.

NATIONAL INCOME AND EXPENDITURE MATRIX

(*£million*)

	Sector	Persons	Firms	Receipts to: Government	Capital	Abroad	Total	
	Persons	—	19,663 (4)	3,810 (5)	1,842 (6)	14 (20)	25,329	Personal expenditure
	Firms	23,099 (1) & (2)	—	4,139 (11) (14) (15) (16) (17)	2,763 (18)		30,001	Gross national expenditure
Payments by	Government	2,230 (3)	5,107 (7)	—	476 (19)	136 (12)	7,949	
	Capital		4,968 (8)		—	113 (13)	5,081	
	Abroad		263 (9) & (10)			—	263	
	Total	25,329	30,001	7,949	5,081	263	—	

| | Personal incomes | Gross national product at market prices | | Total savings | | |

NOTE: The numbers in brackets refer to the correspondingly numbered entries in the social accounts, the bar charts and the flow diagram. It is a good exercise to identify the transactions.

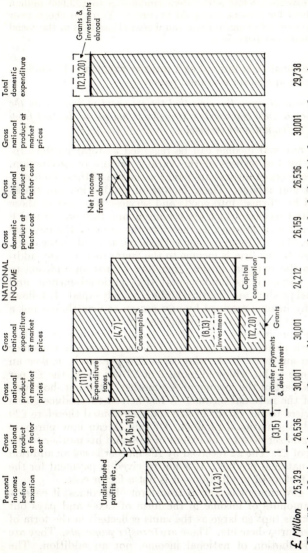

£ Million

FIG. 53.—*National income and expenditure: components of and relationship between the various concepts*

NOTE: The numbers in brackets refer to the correspondingly numbered items in the social accounts, the matrix, and the flow diagram.

For example, what is the item amounting to £23,099 million received by persons and paid by firms? You can check your answer by referring to items numbered (1) and (2) in the social accounts (*see* page 78).

8. National Debt interest as a transfer payment. The following question was set in a final paper:

> *Comment upon the view that the payment of interest on the National Debt represents a transfer payment, as distinct from part of the national income.*

The national income can be regarded as total incomes received by the owners of the various factors of production. The receivers of income are paid for the use of these factors—capital and labour. These factors of production are transformed by "firms" into goods and services; the cost of these goods and services which are produced, and the total of which is the national product, is therefore the same as the national income. The national income is the same as total factor costs. The cost to the firm is income to the factor owner. Any addition to the national income therefore entails an addition to factor costs. It is fundamental that national income and national product are identical and not merely equal. It follows that any income received by any person or firm that is not a factor cost is not part of the national income.

How can incomes arise which are not factor costs? The answer is clear: by the transfer of incomes from one person or firm to another. If A, who earns £20 per week, makes an allowance to his widowed mother of £2 per week, the £2 per week is part of the income of A's mother. It is not, however, part of the national income. A has helped to produce goods or services to the extent of £20 and contributed therefore £20 towards the national product. Of this, A can now purchase goods and services to the extent of £18, and his mother to the extent of £2. The £2 received by A's mother is *not* an addition to the national product. It is not received in payment for the use of factors of production—it is not a factor cost.

The government is a great transferor of incomes; it collects large amounts of income in the form of taxes and pays out large sums (not so large as the sums collected) in the form of social security benefits. These are *transfer payments*. They are a redistribution of national income, not an addition. The same thing is true of interest on National Debt—a redistribution of income from taxpayers to the owners of government securities. This interest is also a transfer payment.

The interest on National Debt is not a factor cost; it is not regarded as payment for newly created services, services which could be transferred from one use to another. The government loans on which the interest is being paid have long since been spent and is not represented for the most part by any capital which provides any income or current services. In so far as the government loans have in turn been lent or invested and interest has been received by the government for the current services of such investments, this interest is already included in the national income and national product in that it is both a cost to the borrowing "firm" and an income to the government. Interest on National Debt is thus a redistribution of incomes.

The concept of national product (which is identical with national income) is an aggregate of goods and services which are currently being produced. The interest on National Debt does *not* add to the value of this aggregate. This can be clearly seen if we consider two countries, both similar in every respect other than that one has a large government debt upon which interest is being paid. We should not consider that the country paying interest on government debt increased that country's national product.

It is possible to conceive of interest on National Debt as payment for the services of continuing to provide loans but such services cannot be transferred to other uses. It is scarcely in the same category as interest paid for the use of capital which can be used to provide goods and services and whose use can be switched from one employment to another.

It is therefore usual to regard payment of interest on the National Debt as a transfer payment, except, of course, in so far as any part is paid to non-residents of a country, any such payment abroad being a deduction from the national income. This payment is not a redistribution of domestic income; it is a deduction from the resources available for use at home.

NOTE: The answer to the question is in essay form. This is the usual way of answering examination questions in economics. Do *not* answer in "note" form.

D 2

9. Difficulties in comparing national incomes. The main difficulties are:

(a) *Over time.*

(i) Changes in money incomes do not measure very accurately changes in real income even when deflated by appropriate price indices.
(ii) Changes in the composition of the national income.
(iii) Changes in the population.
(iv) Changes in the distribution of income.
(v) Leisure is ignored.

(b) *Territorially.*
In addition to all the above:

(vi) Different goods and services enter into the market.
(vii) Does not take into account differences in needs and tastes.
(viii) Different currencies.

PROGRESS TEST 9

1. What is meant by the national income? **(1)**
2. Is income tax part of the national income? **(1, 2)**
3. Are expenditure taxes part of the national income? **(2)**
4. How is the national income measured? **(4)**
5. What is meant by:

(a) Gross national income at factor cost?
(b) Gross national expenditure at market prices?
(c) Gross domestic product?
(d) Gross domestic capital formation?
(e) Gross total domestic expenditure at market prices?
(f) Net investment abroad?
(g) Net national income at factor cost?
(h) Capital consumption? **(2, 4)**

6. Show the relationship between all the concepts in Question 5. **(6)**
7. Show how the various incomes from work and property are at the same time costs which add up to the gross national product? **(5, 3)**
8. What are transfer payments? **(2)**

9. Is National Debt interest a transfer payment? **(8)**

10. What difficulties are there in comparing the national income of a country over time? **(9)**

11. What difficulties are there in comparing the national incomes of two countries? **(9)**

12. What are the effects of grants made to residents abroad upon the gross national product? **(6)**

13. What does (a) domestic investment, (b) investment abroad, consist of? **(2)**

CHAPTER X

TOPICS ON TAXATION

1. Sales tax. Expenditure taxes (outlay taxes), such as customs and excise duties and purchase taxes, are collected from importers, producers or wholesalers. A sales tax (as exists in many other countries) is collected from retailers and covers a much wider selection of goods.

(*a*) *Advantages.*

(i) Does not have the disincentive effect of income tax, and if the levy of a sales tax enabled income tax to be reduced, this would lead to an encouragement of production and saving.

(ii) Small rate of tax would lead to a large amount of revenue. Exemption of tax in case of food would to a large extent nullify the disadvantages mentioned below.

(iii) Changes in the rate of sales tax could be a means of expanding or reducing consumption, hence influencing savings.

(*b*) *Disadvantages.*

(i) Regressive in nature.
(ii) Difficult to administer.

2. Expenditure tax. This is levied on the amount of money spent during the year above a certain exemption limit. It is an alternative to income tax. The advantages of this are:

(*a*) The tax is based upon what a person takes from the national product instead of what is added to it, as is the case with income tax.

(*b*) Expenditure tax can control the economy to an even greater extent than a sales tax.

(*c*) It has a smaller disincentive effect than an income tax.

The method of assessment would be somewhat as follows:

Bank balance at beginning of year

plus

Income during year
Money received as loans or repayment of loans
Sales of investments, including houses

less

Money lent or repaid

Purchase of investments, including houses

less

Bank balance at end of year

equals

Gross expenditure

Gross expenditure

less

Exemption expenditure

equals

Expenditure subject to tax

NOTE: Do not confuse an expenditure tax, which is an alternative to an income tax, with expenditure taxes which are outlay taxes.

3. Raising government income by taxation. The following question appeared in a recent final economics paper:

What taxes would you pose or increase, and what taxes would you avoid, if you wished to add to the income of the government with a minimum of discouragement to the economic activity of the taxpayer?

It is impossible to state the effect of an increase in the rates of income tax upon any particular individual. Some people will work harder to have the same net income as before while others may prefer more leisure and less income. The net result may or may not be a lowering of the level of economic activity. However, the P.A.Y.E. method of tax collection probably means that the level of economic activity is lower than it otherwise would be since the marginal rate of income tax is very much higher than the average or effective rate. It would not, therefore, seem a very good way of obtaining extra revenue by raising income tax rates.

Nevertheless, the experience of the United Kingdom has shown that increased income tax rates have not been followed by a general fall in the level of economic activity. The reason for this is undoubtedly that the increased incomes have more than counteracted the effects of increased rates, in so far as they have tended to decrease the level of economic activity. It would, therefore, be possible to increase income tax rates during a period of increasing incomes *provided the increase in rates does not leave the taxpayer in a less enviable position than before the increase in both income and tax*. This proposition would apply to a tax on both wages and profits.

It is also impossible to say what the effect of increased income tax would be upon the amount of overtime. Here, however, because of the high marginal rate of taxation on overtime earnings (that is the *additional* tax on the *additional* income) and the fact that the worker will already have relatively considerable normal earnings, the general tendency is for additional activity to be discouraged. However, the amount of overtime worked has been continuously increasing since World War II. This is probably due to the increasing materialistic outlook, the growth of the acquisitive mentality and the "hire-purchase" economy that enables such a way of life to become effective. Nevertheless, the effect of such marginal rates has probably had the effect of limiting the increase of economic activity; it would therefore be wise to avoid any increase in income tax rates that affected overtime earnings. A practical difficulty arises in this connection. A person might take time off during his normal hours, subject to increased income tax rates, and make up for lost time by working more overtime, not subject to increased rates. It would not, however, be beyond the ingenuity of the law maker to overcome this.

In so far as a *capital gains tax* is not a tax on gains which are a result of work on the part of the person to whom they accrue, it will have little effect on the level of economic activity. Increased *estate duty* upon the larger estates would increase the revenue without adverse effects upon the level of economic activity. Increasing *taxes on commodities* whose demand is inelastic, or imposing new taxes on commodities not already taxed, will raise government revenue. The resulting increased prices may well give rise to demands for increased wages, but will not in themselves cause a decrease in economic activity.

4. The excess burden of an expenditure tax. It is proposed to show that a taxpayer will be on a higher indifference curve if he pays a certain amount of money in income tax instead of in the form of, say, purchase tax.

In Fig. 54 the quantity of the commodity purchased is shown along the X axis and the money income of the consumer along the Y axis. I_1, I_2 and I_3 are indifference curves. OY is the consumer's income.

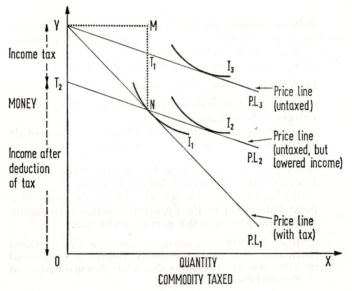

FIG. 54.—*Excess burden of an expenditure tax*

PL_3 is the price line if the consumer is untaxed. The imposition of a purchase tax gives the price line PL_1. YM of the commodity is bought at a cost of MN and the consumer arrives at indifference curve I_1.

YM at the original price would have cost MT_1. T_1N is therefore the amount of taxation. If an equal amount is raised by income tax instead of purchase tax the consumer's income would be OT_2 and the price line PL_2. The consumer would arrive at the indifference curve I_2 (since indifference curves are convex to the origin)—a higher indifference curve than I_1. An income tax, equivalent in amount to a purchase tax, puts the consumer in a more favourable position.

This analysis assumes equal incomes under both methods of taxation. Where, however, the rates of income tax are high, there is little incentive to undertake risks when a large part of the profits, the payment for undertaking risks, is taken away in taxation. It would seem therefore, that incomes would *not* be equal under the two methods.

5. Selective employment tax. This tax is levied upon certain firms in respect of certain employees and thus adds to labour costs. Which firms and which employees are selected will depend upon the economic policies being pursued.

(*a*) *Examples of how selection can be made.*

(i) *According to regions.* In pursuance of a policy to redeploy labour regionally.

(ii) *Taxing firms to raise their labour costs.* To provide an incentive to use more capital in place of labour.

(iii) *Taxing firms with surplus labour.* There is a tendency for firms to have more labour than is necessary—a labour reserve—in times of full employment.

(iv) *Taxing firms in respect of staff engaged on distribution.* This would be the appropriate action if too many people are engaged in this part of production.

NOTE: A selective employment tax is a very powerful instrument of fiscal and economic policy; it is essential therefore that the utmost care should be taken in the selection of firms and class of employees.

(*b*) *Economic effects.* If the tax collected by the government is not spent by them, it will be deflationary and entail the usual results of deflationary measures. If, however, the tax is used solely as a means of raising revenue to meet government expenditure the economic effects will be to change the structure of production and consumption.

PROGRESS TEST 10

1. What is a sales tax? **(1)**

2. What is an expenditure tax? **(2)**

3. How does a government raise revenue by taxation? **(3)**

4. What are the advantages and disadvantages of a sales tax? **(1)**

5. Compare the merits from the *consumer's point of view* of an income tax and an outlay tax. **(4)**

6. How would an expenditure tax be assessed? **(2)**

7. Would it be possible for a government to increase revenue by lowering a purchase tax? **(3)**

8. What effect do the various forms of taxation have upon the willingness of the taxpayer to work? **(3)**

9. What do you understand by a selective employment tax? How can it be used in furtherance of economic policy? **(5)**

10. What are the economic effects of a selective employment tax? **(5)**

CHAPTER XI

MACRO-ECONOMICS

1. Income, consumption and saving. Refer to Fig. 55. Income is shown along the X axis and expenditure along the Y axis.

OO_1 is a line drawn so that any point on it indicates that expenditure is equal to income. The line $LEGI$ shows the amount of expenditure on consumption goods at various incomes; thus, when the income is OY_2, expenditure is Y_2G.

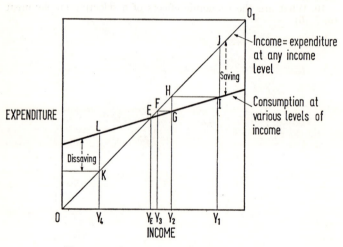

EXPENDITURE

Income = expenditure at any income level

Saving

Consumption at various levels of income

Dissaving

INCOME

FIG. 55.—*Income, consumption and saving*

If the income were OY_1 expenditure would be Y_1I and IJ would therefore be the amount of saving—the difference between income and expenditure on consumption goods.

If the income were OY_4, the amount of expenditure would be Y_4L and there would be a dis-saving of KL; people will either borrow or use past savings.

Let us assume that people spend their income only on consumption goods. An income of OY_1 would mean an expenditure of Y_1I; this would be the income for the following period and equal to OY_2 ($Y_1I = Y_2H = OY_2$). An income of OY_2 would mean an expenditure on consumption goods of Y_2G, the income of the next period and equal to OY_3 ($Y_2G = Y_3F = OY_3$). It will be seen that, so long as expenditure on consumption is less than income, the income of the following period falls until an equilibrium income of OY_E is reached.

Saving appears to lower income and, hence, create unemployment. The solution is investment. But it is not necessarily the answer to make investment just equal to the amount of savings. This would achieve stability, but the level of incomes could still be very low. Any position along the line OO_1 is stable.

The consumers who save are not the persons who invest. Hence there is no reason why planned savings should equal planned investment, which would be necessary for stable employment (*ex-ante* savings = *ex-ante* investment).

> NOTE: Stable employment is not necessarily full employment.
> It was noted in Chapter IX that *ex-post* (that is, after economic forces have worked themselves out) investment is equal to *ex-post* savings. How *ex-ante* inequality becomes *ex-post* equality is explained by means of the multiplier.

2. The multiplier. Any investment (that is, additions to real capital) means incomes to the people who produce it. Part of this additional income will be spent on consumption goods and the remainder will be saved. The amount spent on consumption goods means the production of more consumption goods which means that the producers of *these* additional consumption goods will, in turn, receive incomes. This second set of income receivers will also spend part of *their* income on consumption goods, giving rise to incomes to a third set of income receivers. This process will continue until the total amount of savings (that is, income not spent on consumption goods) is equal to the original investment.

The following example illustrates this: Let an investment of £2500 be made when the marginal propensity to save is $\frac{4}{5}$. This means that $\frac{4}{5}$ of any additional income is saved; that $\frac{1}{5}$ of any additional income is spent on consumption goods (the marginal propensity to spend is $\frac{1}{5}$).

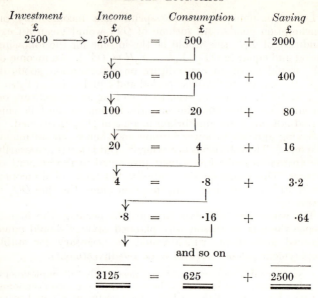

Investment £	Income £		Consumption £		Saving £
2500 ⟶	2500	=	500	+	2000
	500	=	100	+	400
	100	=	20	+	80
	20	=	4	+	16
	4	=	·8	+	3·2
	·8	=	·16	+	·64
			and so on		
	3125	=	625	+	2500

NOTE

(i) Total saving is equal to investment.

(ii) Multiplier $= \dfrac{\text{Total incomes generated}}{\text{Investment}} = \dfrac{3125}{2500} = 1 \cdot 25$

$\qquad\quad = \dfrac{1}{\text{Marginal propensity to save}} = \dfrac{1}{4/5} = 1 \cdot 25$

(iii) The higher the propensity to save, the lower the multiplier.

(iv) The *ex-post* savings are determined by investment; *ex-ante* savings plans are changed as a result of changes in incomes which come about through changes in investment.

The multiplier effect will not, of course, work when there is full employment. Any attempt at investment will require offering higher wages to people who are already in employment. Should such offers succeed in attracting the necessary workmen, all that can happen is that there will be a change in what is produced; there is no increase in output. There is no increase in real incomes; there will, however, be wage-induced inflation.

The multiplier effect can also work in reverse. An increase in savings, not counteracted by an increase in investment, will mean less incomes to the providers of consumption goods, who will, in turn, spend less and this process will continue until there is no excess of savings over investment (*see* Fig. 55).

3. The accelerator. A rise in income means an increased demand for consumption goods. This may lead to further investment-induced investment. In addition there is investment to replace machines which are used up. The relation between changes in demand and changes in investment, which come about because of these changes in demand, is the accelerator.

For example:

(*a*) Machines have a life of four years.

(*b*) Each machine has an output of 2,000,000 pairs of nylon stockings per year.

Year	Demand million pairs	Machines required	Induced	Investment Replacement	Total
1	10	5	5	—	5
2	20	10	5	—	5
3	30	15	5	—	5
4	40	20	5	—	5
5	40	20	—	5	5
6	48	24	4	5	9
7	56	28	4	5	9
8	64	32	4	5	9
9	68	34	2	5	7
10	72	36	2	9	11
11	72	36	—	9	9

The firm commenced manufacturing nylon stockings in year 1 and acquired five machines. The demand for year 2 increased and it was necessary to purchase further machines. The story of the first eleven years of the firm's life is shown in the table above.

It will be seen that in year 5, the machines bought in year 1 have to be replaced. The investment in year 6, consisting of nine machines—induced investment of four machines and replacement investment of five machines—having a life of 4 years, are replaced in year 10. Similarly, *total* investment in year 7 becomes *replacement* investment in year 11.

From the data relating to the demand for stockings, and the corresponding investment required, the following table has been drawn up showing the relationship between changes in demand and changes in investment.

	Change in demand		Change in investment	
	absolute			
	million	rate	absolute	rate
Year	pairs	%	machines	%
2	+10	+100	nil	nil
3	+10	+50	nil	nil
4	+10	+33⅓	nil	nil
5	nil	nil	nil	nil
6	+8	+20	+4	+80
7	+8	+16⅔	nil	nil
8	+8	+14³⁄₇	nil	nil
9	+4	+6¼	−2	−22²⁄₉
10	+4	+5¹⁵⁄₁₇	+4	+57¹⁄₇
11	nil	nil	−2	−18²⁄₁₁

From year 1 to year 4, in order to maintain a constant level of investment, it has been necessary for the demand to increase by a constant amount each year. Note that during this time the whole of the investment was induced.

From then on, had demand remained constant at 40,000,000, investment would have been maintained at a constant level—but then the whole of investment would have been replacement investment.

However, in year 6, demand increased and there is a new level of investment. Demand increased by 20%, but investment increased by 80%. To maintain this new level of investment demand had to increase by equal amounts each year, which was the case for years 7 and 8. In year 9, although demand increased, it increased by a lesser amount than the previous years (only 4 million as against 8 million) and investment fell.

In year 10, although demand increased by the same amount as year 9, an increase of 5¹⁵⁄₁₇% in demand gave rise to an investment increase of 57¹⁄₇%. This was due to increased replacement investment. Finally, year 11 saw no increased demand and investment fell. The accelerator and the multiplier reinforce each other (*see* Fig. 56).

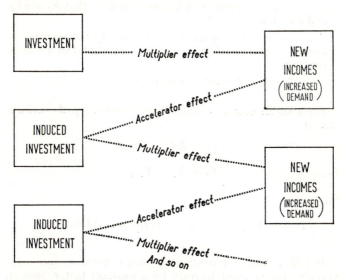

FIG. 56.—*The "chain" reaction of multiplier and accelerator*

4. The warranted rate of growth. Investment (more capital per worker) is necessary for the attainment of a higher national income. It is also necessary to balance investment against savings (which as people get higher incomes will increase) to maintain level of national income. Investment may arise from:

(*a*) Technical progress.
(*b*) Increased demand for goods and services (accelerator principle).

Saving mainly depends on *level of incomes* but *investment* on *growth of income* (anticipated or actual). This can be shown:

Let: I_t be investment in period t.
$\quad\quad Y_t$ be income in period t.
$\quad\quad S_t$ be savings in period t.

I_{t-1}, Y_{t-1}, and S_{t-1} be investment, income and savings for the previous period.

s be proportion of income saved so that $S_t = sY_t$, and let s remain constant.

g be the proportion of the anticipated increase in income invested so that $I_t = g(Y_t - Y_{t-1})$, and let g remain constant.

I_t will, of course, be equal to S_t.

For a stable economy, planned investment equals savings, that is:

$$sY_t = g(Y_t - Y_{t-1})$$

i.e.
$$\frac{s}{g}Y_t = Y_t - Y_{t-1}$$

Similarly:

$$\frac{s}{g}Y_{t+1} = Y_{t+1} - Y_t \quad (t + 1 \text{ is the period following } t)$$

It follows that for continuous growth between successive periods, income must increase by a constant factor, that is, income must increase geometrically, each increase in income being greater than the last.

(a) EXAMPLE 1

Period	Expected income	Increase in income
t	144	—
$t + 1$	180	36
$t + 2$	225	45

NOTE

(i) Income has increased geometrically by a constant ratio of $\frac{5}{4}$.

(ii) $\frac{s}{g} = \frac{1}{5}$; the increase in income is one-fifth of current income.

(b) EXAMPLE 2

Let $s = \dfrac{1}{8}$ and $g = \dfrac{5}{8}$, i.e. $\dfrac{s}{g} = \dfrac{1}{5}$.

Period	Expected income	Savings	Investment	Consumption
t	144	18 ($\frac{1}{8} \times 144$)	18	126
$t + 1$	180	22·5 ($\frac{1}{8} \times 180$)	22·5 ($\frac{5}{8} \times 36$)	157·5
$t + 2$	200	25 ($\frac{1}{8} \times 200$)	12·5 ($\frac{5}{8} \times 20$)	175

In the first example, income increases are a constant proportion of current income, namely $\frac{1}{5}$. This is the *warranted rate of growth*. This is the rate of growth which makes planned investment equal to planned savings. Expected incomes become actual incomes. This is the requirement for stable growth.

In the second example, the rate of growth for period $t + 2$ was below the warranted rate of growth—200 instead of 225. Planned investment was less than planned savings and, hence, *realised income was* 187·5 (175 consumption + 12·5 investment) as against an expected income of 200. It follows that investment for period $t + 3$ will fall. Income instead of rising will start to fall until saving and investment are in equilibrium.

NOTE: Actual increase in income for period $t + 2$ was 7·5. Voluntary investment is $\frac{5}{8}$ of 7·5 = $4\frac{11}{16}$. Involuntary investment is $12\frac{1}{2} - 4\frac{11}{16} = 7\frac{13}{16}$.

PROGRESS TEST 11

1. What is meant by the warranted rate of growth? (**4**)

2. What is meant by investment and what gives rise to it? (**2** and **4**)

3. What is the effect of saving upon the national income? (**1**)

4. What do you understand by the multiplier? When does the multiplier effect cease to work? (**2**)

5. Define the marginal propensity to save. What is its relation to the multiplier? (**2**)

6. How does *ex-ante* inequality of planned savings and planned investment become *ex-post* equality of savings and investment? (**2**)

7. Explain the accelerator effect. (**3**)

8. What is the relation, if any, between the accelerator and the multiplier? (3)

9. Both savings and investment depend upon incomes, but not in the same way. Comment. (4)

10. What happens if the national income increases at a rate less than its warranted rate of growth? (4)

11. What is the relation between income, consumption, saving and investment? (1, 2, 4)

CHAPTER XII

THE THEORY OF INTERNATIONAL TRADE

1. Production possibilities under increasing costs. All production is finally subject to the law of diminishing marginal productivity and hence increasing costs. This is a fundamental law of economics and should have been mastered in an intermediate course. (See Chapter III, *Basic Economics*, Macdonald and Evans.)

Below is given:

(*a*) A table showing the production of seed potatoes which varies according to the number of men working for eight hours a day for a given number of weeks on, say, an acre of land.

(*b*) A table showing the production of oats according to the number of men working for eight hours a day for the same number of weeks as on the production of potatoes, also on an acre of land.

(i) *Production of seed potatoes according to the Law of diminishing marginal productivity.*

Units of variable factor (*men*)	Total product (*tons*)	Marginal product (*tons*)
0	0	0
1	6	6
2	18	12
3	33	15
4	40	7
5	45	5
6	48	3
7	49	1

(This example is taken from *Basic Economics*, Chapter III, **4**, which gives a detailed explanation of the Law of diminishing marginal productivity.)

(ii) *Production of oats according to the Law of diminishing marginal productivity*.

Units of variable factor (men)	Total product (bushels)	Marginal product (bushels)
0	0	0
1	14	14
2	30	16
3	50	20
4	65	15
5	75	10
6	80	5
7	82	2

However, if some of the men—the variable factor—spend their time producing potatoes and the remainder oats, then various combinations of potatoes and oats can be produced with a given total amount of men as shown in the table below, which is compiled from the two previous tables.

(iii) *Production possibilities*.

Units of variable factor used for producing		Total product		Marginal rate of transformation
Seed potatoes (men)	Oats (men)	Seed potatoes (tons)	Oats (bushels)	
7	0	49	0	—
6	1	48	14	1/14
5	2	45	30	3/16
4	3	40	50	5/20
3	4	33	65	7/15
2	5	18	75	15/10
1	6	6	80	12/5
0	7	0	82	6/2

An example from the table (iii) gives six men producing potatoes and one man oats, a total production of 48 tons of seed potatoes and 14 bushels of oats; another example gives three men producing potatoes and four men oats, a total production of 33 tons of potatoes and 65 bushels of oats.

All the possibilities can be shown graphically as in Fig. 57, which gives the *production possibility curve* for the above example.

The last column of the *production possibilities* table, headed *marginal rate of transformation* shows the ratio of *loss* in production of potatoes (due to employing one less man on their production) to *gain* in production of oats (due to employing one more man on their production).

For example, employing four instead of five men on the production of potatoes, and three instead of two on the production of oats, means a *loss* of 5 tons of seed potatoes (40 instead of 45) and a *gain* of 20 bushels of oats (50 instead of 30). The marginal rate of transformation is 5/20.

It will be noted that the marginal rate of transformation increases—more and more seed potatoes must be given up for

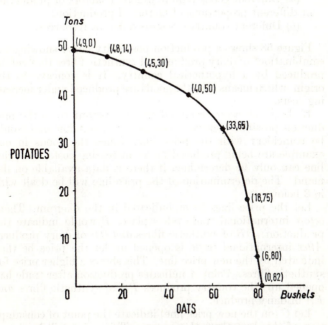

FIG. 57.—*A production possibility curve*

E

less and less oats. Oats are becoming dearer and dearer in terms of seed potatoes, that is, they are being produced under increasing costs. It will also be observed that the marginal rate of transformation indicates the slope of the production possibility curve and this becomes steeper and steeper; it is concave to the origin. This is the shape of a production possibility curve of goods being produced under increasing costs.

2. International trade under increasing costs. International trade takes place because the production possibility curves (also known as *transformation curves*) vary from country to country. This is another way of saying that international trade arises because comparative costs are not the same in all countries.

Production possibility curves differ because:

(*a*) Different goods require different factors of production or different proportions of factors of production.

(*b*) Different countries possess different resources.

Figure 58 shows a production possibility curve showing the combinations of dairy produce and synthetic fibres that can be produced by a hypothetical country. It is concave to the origin, which means that the goods are produced under increasing costs.

If the goods were produced under constant costs the production possibility curve would be a straight line *and* would be coincident with the price line. Since the goods in our example are being produced under increasing costs, the price line can only be determined if there is data available on demand. The determination of the price line will be dealt with in **3** below.

Let the price lines be as indicated in the diagram. Then, *before* international trade takes place, *B* would indicate the production; *DB* of synthetic fibres *and* *QB* of dairy produce. *After* international trade is opened up let the price be that indicated by the new price line. This shows a higher price for synthetic fibres. Point *A* indicates production after trade has opened up; the country produces *PA* of synthetic fibres *and* *FA* of dairy produce.

Let *C* (on the new price line) indicate the point of consumption of this hypothetical country. (This point will be deter-

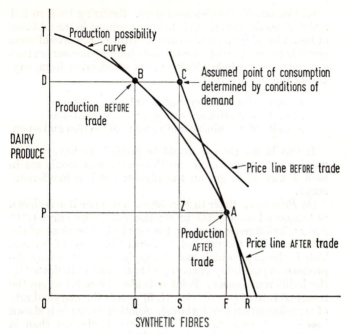

FIG. 58.—*Effect of international trade upon production*

mined by the conditions of demand and will be dealt with in **3** below.) Then the country will export *ZA* of synthetic fibres and import *ZC* of dairy produce. It has produced *FA* of dairy produce and imported *ZC*, giving a total of *SC* (since *FA* = *SZ*) and this equals *QB*, the same consumption as before international trade. However, it has *DC* of synthetic fibres (it produced *PA*, exported *ZA*, leaving *PZ* = *DC*) instead of only *DB*.

The country is therefore in a better position after international trade than before.

3. Terms of trade. The most important factors to consider are:

(*a*) *Community indifference curves.* Referring back to I, **1** and **2**, it would seem that there is no meaning in the addition of individuals' indifference curves. However, it would seem possible to conceive of a community indifference curve; that a country as a whole obtains equal satisfaction from, say, any of the combinations:

x_1 units of machinery *and* y_1 units of textiles *or*
x_2 units of machinery *and* y_2 units of textiles *or*
x_3 units of machinery *and* y_3 units of textiles and so on.

If this be so, then it would be possible to have a community indifference map and the community would act in such a way as to get on the highest possible indifference curve.

(*b*) *Price line.* Refer to Fig. 59(*a*). The price line is shown as tangential to both the production possibility curve (*PP*) and an indifference curve at the point *G*. The slope of the price line gives the price of machinery in terms of textiles. This is the price which makes *supply*, as indicated by the production possibility curve, *equal to demand*, as indicated by the indifference curve. Point *G* is also the point where the marginal rate of substitution (I, **3**) equals the marginal rate of transformation (*see* **1** above). Another example is shown in Fig. 59(*b*)—the price of machinery is cheaper than in Fig. 59(*a*), the slope is not so steep (II, **2**).

NOTE: The two examples just given were before trade took place between the nations, that is, for closed economies.

(*c*) *Terms of trade.* Refer to Fig. 59. Sections (*a*) and (*b*) show the determination of the price lines of the two countries "Gallia" and "Anglia" and points *G* and *A* show their respective productions when there is no trade between them.

After trade has opened up between the two countries, the position is indicated in Fig. 59, sections (*c*) and (*d*). They show:

    (i) The determination of the price line, which must be the same for both countries if there is trade between them (ignoring transport costs dealt with in **4**).

(ii) The production of the two countries.
(iii) The amounts of textiles and machinery exported and imported.

The price line is indicated by *TC* and *LH*. They are parallel, that is, they have the same slope showing that the price is the same in both countries. This price is between the two *closed economy* prices.

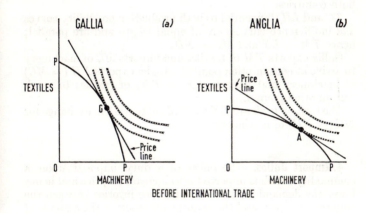

BEFORE INTERNATIONAL TRADE

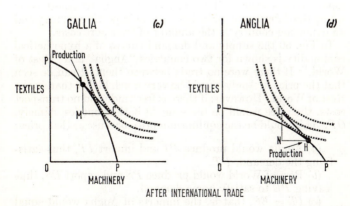

AFTER INTERNATIONAL TRADE

FIG. 59.—*Terms of trade*

The production levels of the two countries are indicated by points T and H. Gallia now produces more textiles and less machinery, and Anglia more machinery and less textiles than before. This is because Gallia had the comparative advantage in producing textiles, and Anglia had the comparative advantage in producing machinery.

C and L are the respective consumption points. They are on higher indifference curves than points G and A of the closed economies. International trade has improved the position of both countries.

TC and LH (tangential to both production possibility curves *and* indifference curves) are of equal length and are parallel; hence $TM = LN$ and $MC = NH$.

Gallia exports TM of textiles and imports MC of machinery to arrive at consumption point C. Anglia exports NH ($= MC$) of machinery and imports LN ($= TM$) of textiles to reach consumption point L.

The *terms of trade* are LN ($= TM$) of textiles in exchange for MC ($= NH$) of machinery.

4. Import duties. The effect of a duty imposed upon a commodity which is imported is to increase its price and hence lower the demand for it. The difference in price between the country of export and the country of import is the amount of duty. This is exactly the same, in effect, as transport costs where the difference in price between an importing country and an exporting country is the amount of transport costs.

In Fig. 60 the supply and demand curves of a hypothetical commodity is shown for two countries "Anglia" and "Rest of World." If there were no trade between them, it can be seen that the price in Anglia would be very much higher than in the Rest of World. However, if there is free trade and no transport costs, the price would be the same in both countries, namely, OP. This would be the equilibrium price because at that price:

(a) Anglia would produce PI and import IT, thus satisfying the demand, PT.

(b) Rest of World would produce PS and export ES, thus leaving PE to satisfy home demand.

(c) $IT = ES$, that is, the imports of Anglia would equal the exports of Rest of World.

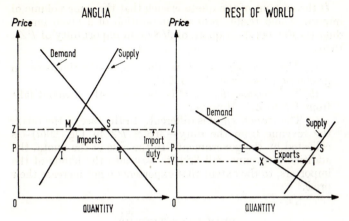

FIG. 60.—*Effect of tariffs on international trade*

The effect of international trade has been to lower price in Anglia and raise it in Rest of World. If an import duty is now imposed in Anglia, the equilibrium price is OZ in Anglia and OY in Rest of World, a difference of ZY, being the amount of duty per unit of the commodity. These prices are equilibrium prices because:

(*a*) Anglia would produce ZM (more than before the tariff was imposed) and import MS, thus satisfying the demand of ZS.

(*b*) Rest of World would produce YT and export XT, thus leaving YX to satisfy home demand.

(*c*) $MS = XT$, that is, the imports of Anglia equal the exports of Rest of World, but there is less trade than before the duty was imposed.

NOTE: The same argument and diagrams would be used if there were transport costs. ZY in Fig. 60 would then be the cost of transport, per unit of commodity.

5. Import duties *v.* quotas. An alternative method to imposing an import duty in order to restrict imports is to fix the quantity of imports allowed, that is, to fix a *quota*.

If the amount of the quota is such that the same volume of imports would result from the imposition of a given import duty (in Fig. 60(*a*)—a quota of *MS* or an import duty of *PZ*), then:

(*a*) The *protective effect* is the *same*—the increase in production rises from *PI* to *ZM*.

(*b*) The *consumption effect* is the *same*—the demand falls from *PT* to *ZS*. However:

(*c*) The *revenue effect* is different. In the case of the tariff, the revenue from the duty—*MS* × *PZ* in Fig. 60(*a*)—is collected by the government. In the case of the quota, the additional revenue will find its way into the hands of the importers, to the extent that exporters do not increase their price.

PROGRESS TEST 12

1. What is meant by the marginal rate of transformation? (**1**)

2. Would a production possibility curve enable: (*a*) The *actual* amount of production to be known. (*b*) The price to be determined? If not, what further information is required? (**3**)

3. What do you understand by the terms of trade and how are they determined? (**3**)

4. What is the difference, in effect, between an import duty and a quota which raises the price by the same amount? (**5**)

5. What is: (*a*) The protective effect. (*b*) The consumption effect. (*c*) The effect on prices, of: (i) An import duty. (ii) Transport costs? (**4, 5**)

6. Show how international trade benefits a country? (**2, 3**)

7. Show how a production possibility curve can be obtained. (**1**)

8. What do you understand by a community indifference curve? (**3**)

9. How is a price line determined under conditions of increasing costs? (**3**)

CHAPTER XIII

PROBLEMS OF FOREIGN TRADE

Chapters XIX and XX of "Basic Economics" must be thoroughly revised.

1. Balance of payments. Below is the balance of payments for the United Kingdom for 1964. Particular attention should be paid to the effect of the monetary movements (how the balance is settled) on the external liabilities of the U.K.

United Kingdom Balance of Payments, 1964	£m.	£m.
Current account		
Imports	5005	
Exports	4471	
Visible balance—unfavourable	——	534
Invisible balance—favourable		122
CURRENT BALANCE—unfavourable		412
Long-term capital account		
Inter-government loans (net)—payments	101	
Private investment		
Abroad	398	
In the United Kingdom	170	
	—— 228	
Other official long-term capital—payments	15	
	——	344
Balancing item		−35
BALANCE ON CURRENT AND LONG-TERM CAPITAL ACCOUNT		721
Monetary movements		
Change in gold and convertible currency reserves—fall	£m.	122
Drawings from the I.M.F.		359
Changes in liabilities in non-sterling currencies (net):		
United Kingdom banks		138
Assistance received from overseas central banks		72
Changes in external liabilities in sterling		−6
Other miscellaneous short-term items		36
BALANCE OF MONETARY MOVEMENTS		721

The effect of the monetary movements has been (*a*) to decrease gold and currency reserves and (*b*) to increase external liabilities over the year as shown below:

Gold and currency reserves	£m.	*International Monetary Fund*	£m.
End 1963	949	Sterling holdings end	
Less fall	122	1963	522
	——	*Add* drawings 1964	359
End 1964	827		——
		Sterling holdings end	
		1964	881

External liabilities and claims in non-sterling currencies—United Kingdom banks	£m.	*United Kingdom external liabilities and claims in sterling (excluding I.M.F.)*	£m.
Net liabilities end 1963	11	Net liabilities end 1963	3176
Add increase	138	*Less* decrease 1964	6
Net liabilities end 1964	149	Net liabilities end 1964	3170

2. Monetary policy and the balance of payments.

The following question was set in a final paper:

Explain how changes in the monetary policy of a country may influence its balance of payments.

The monetary policy of a country is directed towards securing and maintaining the "right" amount of money. The right amount of money is that amount which will enable stable prices to be maintained and full employment to be secured without introducing "balance of payments" difficulties. Often, however, balance of payments considerations are the cause of changes in monetary policy. Then, the policy must be one that, while alleviating the balance of payments weakness, does not disturb the internal equilibrium. On the other hand, monetary policy may be directed towards obtaining or maintaining internal equilibrium, correcting inflation or securing full employment. Any measures in this direction will normally have repercussions on the balance of payments. It is therefore necessary when considering monetary policy to envisage the effects on both internal and external equilibrium before the appropriate changes in policy can be determined and the appropriate method or methods adopted.

The monetary authorities may decide to change the Bank Rate. The purpose of this is to change the short-term interest rates, for all short-term rates will follow bank-rate changes. These changes in short-term rates will lead to changes in the amount of bank loans and hence the amount of money. The aim of changing the Bank Rate was once to influence the inflows and outflows of gold, any influence upon the commercial banks' deposits being incidental. A rise in the interest rates causes foreigners to make short-term loans and there is a corresponding inflow of gold. It is doubtful whether this is an improvement in the balance of payments, even though there is an increase in the gold and convertible currencies reserves. At the moment of writing there is much "hot money" which foreigners have invested here because of the high Bank Rate. The high interest payments are an expensive way of increasing reserves which will be depleted when the interest rate falls. It is better not to consider short loans of other than a monetary movement as, in fact, is done in the official balance of payments accounts.

However, the change in the Bank Rate is nowadays intended, in addition to influencing gold flows, to increase or contract the amount of bank credit. Often this act is reinforced by open-market operations. It is now considered doubtful how far the Bank Rate and open-market operations are effective, at any rate to curb inflation and to restrict credit and for this reason a *special deposit* system is now operating. The consequent change in the amount of money will change the price level internally. If, for example, the effect of the restriction of credit has the effect of lowering the price level of goods in, say, country A, then, providing the prices in country B do not change, and provided the sum of the elasticities of demand are greater than unity, and further that the exchange rate does not change, the result will be an improvement in the balance of payments of country A. In point of fact, there is little chance of the price level falling in this country as a result of the recent restrictions in credit; the object was to prevent further increases in prices which has the effect of rapidly causing a deterioration in the balance of payments unless prices in other countries are rising equally rapidly. The changes in internal price level brought about by monetary policy have exactly the same effect as changes in exchange rates upon the balance of payments.

A more efficient method than open-market operations of restricting credit is by means of "funding." The monetary authorities, including the Treasury and the Bank of England, put fewer short-term securities on the market and more long-dated. A larger proportion of government bonds are held outside the commercial banking system and this restricts credit considerably and will therefore have more effect on the price level than changes in the Bank Rate or open-market operations. Hence it is more likely to influence the balance of payments. One other effect of funding is a rise in the long-term interest rates. These higher rates may induce long-term capital to flow into the country or may reduce an outflow. This would mean an amelioration in the balance of payments.

A final way of restricting credit is by means of controls, for example, hire purchase restrictions. In so far as restrictions of credit lower prices, the influence upon the balance of payments will be favourable.

Often a fall in prices will affect the level of activity; output and incomes will fall. The fall in incomes will decrease the demand for imports; an improvement in the balance of payments will follow. A rise in output and incomes may easily add to balance of payments difficulties.

NOTE: *Special deposits* are those which commercial banks hold at the Bank of England. They are illiquid and cannot be turned into cash on demand. The greater the ratio of special deposits to ordinary commercial bank deposits at the Bank of England, the less is the cash basis on which commercial banks can create credit.

3. The foreign trade multiplier. A favourable balance on the current account of the balance of payments, that is an excess of exports over imports, acts in the same way as investment upon income and the foreign trade multiplier is completely analogous to the "domestic" multiplier.

Let us suppose that there is a favourable balance on current account of £100, that is, there is an excess of exports over imports of £100. This £100 will give rise to incomes of £100 in the exporting country. Part of this will be spent on consumption goods, part will be saved and part will be spent on imports.

The part spent at home on consumption goods will give rise to a second round of new incomes which in turn will be spent on consumption goods, saved or spent on imports. Again, the part spent on consumption goods at home will give rise to a third round of incomes. This will continue until savings equals the export surplus.

It can be shown that the foreign trade multiplier =

$$\frac{1}{\text{Marginal propensity to } \textit{import} + \text{Marginal propensity to } \textit{save}}$$

NOTE: The accelerator effect on increased incomes has been ignored and also the multiplier effect on any induced investment. Increased incomes of the exporters of goods imported will probably mean increased exports. This has also been ignored. The marginal propensity to import is the proportion of new income spent on imports.

4. International liquidity. This refers to the amount of money available for settling international transactions. The present system requires that countries have reserves of gold and foreign currencies; they settle their indebtedness to other countries by means of either a transfer of gold, or payment in their own or foreign currencies.

The following problems arise:

(*a*) Large-scale movements of funds between countries for speculative purposes can cause balance of payments difficulties.

(*b*) Inadequate growth of monetary reserves in relation to the growth of international trade.

(*c*) Danger to countries holding large exchange reserves.

5. Speculative funds. Large-scale movements of "hot" money come about because of international differences in interest rates or because of rumours of devaluation. The size of the reserves of the countries concerned are often considered inadequate to deal with these movements.

The present practice of some central banks which insist on maintaining low interest rates to help unemployment, even if it leads to a heavy outflow of funds, or, on the other hand, insist upon high interest rates to fight inflation, even though it leads to a heavy inflow of foreign funds, follows a policy in which the rate of interest is used to control employment and growth. At one time central banks adjusted interest rates to keep the balance of payments in equilibrium.

6. Inadequate reserves. It is suggested that, since the ratio of reserves to imports has fallen from 81% in 1950 to 50% in 1960, reserves are inadequate. But the fact that the ratio has fallen does not indicate what should be the right ratio. In 1913 it was 21%.

7. Danger to countries holding large exchange reserves. In many countries, a large part of their reserves consist of foreign exchange, particularly dollars and sterling. The demand for gold for speculation and hedging has meant an increase in the supply of dollars. Since not all central banks will exchange gold for further dollars, the monetary authorities in America have had to sell gold to preserve the gold parity of the dollar. This increases the fear that the gold-exchange standard might collapse. One of the results of such a collapse would be the elimination of key-currencies, dollars and sterling, from the official reserves of central banks and, consequently, a drastic reduction in "liquidity."

8. Overcoming the difficulties. The various plans to overcome these difficulties take the form of:

(a) Co-operation between the central banks or:
(b) Creation of reserves by an expanded I.M.F. or:
(c) Increase in the price of gold or:
(d) Flexible exchange rates.

9. Co-operation between the central banks.

(a) The bank requiring foreign currency would obtain it from another central bank in return for its own currency.

(b) The I.M.F. acts as an intermediary between the lending and borrowing bank.

A central bank makes a loan to the I.M.F. of a particular currency and the I.M.F. sells this currency to another central bank against its currency. The aim of this support action is to provide finance for a country suffering from a heavy outflow of short-term capital. The proposals for this kind of action provide that those industrial countries with balance of payments surpluses make loans to the I.M.F., so that finance is available for those countries suffering from outflows of short-term capital.

10. Creation of reserves by a revised I.M.F.

(a) *The Triffin plan* would require each member country to hold at least one-fifth of its monetary reserves in the form of deposits with the I.M.F. It would provide for overdraft facilities for central banks. It would also enable the I.M.F. to purchase or sell securities in the open market (the seller of the security deposits the I.M.F.'s cheque with his bank, who deposits it with its central bank, who in turn deposits it with the I.M.F.). The I.M.F. would virtually become a central bank for central banks.

Extract from balance sheet of a revised I.M.F.

Deposits of central banks	Gold and national currencies Securities Overdrafts to central banks

(b) *The Stamp plan* proposes that the I.M.F. should issue certificates to the extent of $3000 million, to be distributed to the governments of the underdeveloped countries. The central banks of countries willing to accept these certificates in payment for exports, would use them as monetary reserves. There would be no need to make them redeemable in gold if they were accepted in payment by most of the member countries of the I.M.F. and could be used for payments to other member countries.

Extract from balance sheet of a revised I.M.F.

Certificates	Debts of under-developed countries

(c) *The "CRU" plan.* The purpose of the plan is to increase monetary reserves by some $2000 million per year. It proposes an international currency, the CRU (collective reserve unit), backed by the national currencies of the participating countries, who would undertake to accept the units from each other in settling accounts. It will not be tied to gold and the number of units that any country would have to take is limited.

11. Increase in the price of gold. An increase in the price of gold would have the effect of raising the value of existing gold reserves. Its increased price, moreover, would cause an increase in gold production and at the higher price would mean a considerably higher annual increase in gold reserves.

The future supply of reserves would no longer depend on sterling and dollar liabilities, which would be eliminated from existing reserves. The revaluation of gold reserves would enable the United Kingdom and America to repurchase the foreign exchange holdings of the other countries and the increase in annual supply would enable the world to do without future accumulations of foreign exchange as monetary reserves.

12. Flexible exchange rates. If exchange rates are allowed to move freely in response to the supply of, and demand for currencies, no balance of payments problem arises. Gold and foreign currency reserves are only needed if exchange rates are fixed and not allowed to move to an equilibrium rate.

With fixed rates, if they lead to a "fundamental disequilibrium" and become "unrealistic," adjustment must ultimately be made. The question arises whether it is better to have occasional adjustments such as devaluation and keep the difficulties that arise with fixed exchange rates or to have the continuous adjustment of flexible exchange rates.

PROGRESS TEST 13

1. How might a large unfavourable balance on the current and long-term capital account of the balance of payments be settled? (1)

2. What are the special deposits held by commercial banks? (2)

3. Compare the relative efficiencies of open-market operations and funding as a means of restricting credit. (2)

4. What is the foreign trade multiplier and how is it calculated? (3)

5. What is the effect of monetary policy upon the balance of payments? (2)

6. What is meant by the marginal propensity to import? (3)

7. What is the effect of monetary movements in settlement of the balance of payments on the monetary assets and liabilities of the United Kingdom. (1)

8. What is meant by international liquidity? How could it be increased? **(4, 8)**

9. What problems arise in the present system of settling international indebtedness? **(4)**

10. How can central banks assist each other to prevent "hot money" causing balance of payments difficulties? **(9)**

11. Describe the Triffin and the Stamp plans for increasing monetary reserves. **(10)**

12. State the case for flexible exchange rates. **(12)**

13. What would be the effect on the gold and currency reserves of central banks if the price of gold was raised? **(11)**

BIBLIOGRAPHY

Economic theory

BOULDING, K. E. *Economic analysis.* Hamish Hamilton.
BROOMAN, F. S. *Macro-economics.* Allen and Unwin.

Price theory

STIGLER, G. J. *The theory of price.* Macmillan.

Trade cycles

MATTHEWS, R. C. O. *The trade cycle.* Nisbet: Cambridge University Press.

Income and expenditure

EDEY AND PEACOCK. *National income and social accounting.* Hutchinson's University Library.

International trade

HARROD, SIR ROY. *International economics.* Nisbet: Cambridge University Press.
HABERLER, G. *A survey of international trade theory.* Princeton University.
KINDLEBERGER. *International economics.* Richard D. Irwin, Inc.

Money

DACEY, W. M. *The British banking mechanism.* Hutchinson.
DAY, A. *The economics of money.* Oxford University Press.
SAYERS, R. S. *Modern banking.* Oxford University Press.
TEW, B. *International monetary co-operation.* Hutchinson's University Library.

Public finance

PREST, A. R. *Public finance in theory and practice.* Weidenfeld and Nicolson.

BIBLIOGRAPHY

EXAMINATION TECHNIQUE

SOME students consider that examinations in economics can be passed by "flannelling"; others think it is only a matter of common sense (which is, in fact, a scarce commodity); and some think that all that is necessary is to read the "serious" newspapers.

This is not so. The *first requisite* for examination success is to *know your subject*.

A large number of students find it easy to understand economics and hence think nothing need be learned. It is too late when you find your memory has failed you in the examination room. You must, therefore, *learn and continually revise* (this book is compiled in such a way as to enable you to do just that).

Often a student fails to check his knowledge as he continues his studies. He then comes up against unnecessary difficulties because he has erroneous ideas about the subject or has failed to learn some vital step. And, of course, if he does not check his knowledge he will not know if he has forgotten some very necessary information for examination success; he will not know if his answers in the examination are right or not.

Test yourself by means of the Progress Tests. It is not sufficient to just look at a question and say, "Oh yes! I know that one." This might merely mean that the question is understood, or that the student remembers having dealt with the subject-matter of the question. *Write out the answer without reference to textbook or notes and then check.*

But, having fully prepared yourself for the examination (examiners report that *many* students fail to prepare adequately), it is still possible to fail. There is, in fact, an examination technique.

The following slogan might be useful to remember when dealing with any question: *answer the question, the whole question, and nothing but the question.*

"Answer the question" might seem superfluous advice, but too often a question is misread and an entirely different question actually answered. However good *this* answer, it cannot earn marks. It is tantamount to saying to the examiner, "I don't know the answer to your question so I have written an answer to a question I do know." *Read the question carefully and make sure you understand it before attempting an answer*.

"The whole question." A question often consists of more than one part. Check that you have answered all the examiner has asked for.

"Nothing but the question": irrelevancies earn no marks and cost time; a most uneconomic policy. There is a tendency to expand an answer on that part about which most is known. This leads to overstepping the limits of the subject to be dealt with. So do *keep to the point*.

Examination procedure.

(1) *Read the instructions carefully and follow them absolutely*. Note particularly the number of questions to be done, and if any are compulsory.

(2) *Allocate your time*. If, for example, the time allowed is two hours and five questions carrying equal marks have to be done, there would be 24 minutes for each question. But of this 24 minutes, perhaps 3 minutes might be required for planning your answer and another 3 minutes for reading it through when completed.

Do not spend more than your allotted time on any question. If it is not completed in that time leave a space and go on to another question. Come back to it if you can gain time on the other questions. More marks are obtained on two half-answered questions than on one completely answered question. The number of marks earned for each minute spent on any question is subject to the law of diminishing returns.

(3) *Decide which question you will answer first*. This will be the one you can answer most confidently. Don't worry about the others. Answering the first question well—and there must be at least one you can answer well if you have paid some attention to your course—will settle "examination nerves."

(4) *Plan the answer to this question*. Jot down all the points that occur to you. Some will possibly be irrelevant; cross them out. Put the others in a logical order. Usually there will only be about three of four points. Devote a paragraph to each one. Choose a good introductory sentence or two and end with a good summary or conclusion. Time spent on planning is well

spent. It ensures that your answer covers the question and does not contain irrelevant topics. It also enables you to give a logically developed answer; this earns marks.

(5) *Write the answer to the question.* Make sure you do not overstep the allocated time. Many students work best when working "against the clock."

(6) *Read your answer.* When reading it imagine yourself to be the examiner. Be critical and correct errors. This step, often neglected, is *very* important. It is so easy to write one thing and intend to write something entirely different. Leaving out a word, *e.g.* "not," may have the effect of turning a "pass" into a failure.

(7) *Pass on to the next question.* Read carefully, plan, write, and read over your answer.

(8) *Continue in this way until all requisite questions are answered.*

(9) *Complete any answers left unfinished.* If there is not sufficient time to complete any answer, finish it in note form or indicate how the answer would be completed. This will often earn useful marks.

Use of diagrams. Use diagrams wherever they can make a useful contribution to your answer. They must be neat and add to the clarity of the answer. But if a diagram gains marks quickly, remember that an incorrect diagram—and particularly a meaningless one—will lose marks equally quickly. Do not add a diagram if it adds nothing to your answer.

TEST PAPERS

Do not attempt these papers until you have thoroughly mastered the course and are able to answer satisfactorily all the progress tests. Do each paper under *strict examination conditions.* Allow *three* hours for each paper. Answer *six* questions.

TEST 1

1. Would an all-round increase in the salaries of civil servants cause the national income, as it is now measured, to rise?

2. Describe and criticise any proposal with which you are acquainted for increasing international liquidity.

3. Examine the desirability of substituting an overall sales tax for the present system of purchase tax.

4. State why the net earnings of a monopoly for its shareholders are described by some as profit and by others as rent.

5. Economists sometimes divide inventions into "labour-saving" and "capital-saving." What is the significance of this distinction?

6. A monopoly is stable; a competitive industry is not. Discuss.

7. What factors mainly determine the bargaining power of either side in a wage dispute?

8. An increase in investment is held to have a multiplier effect on national income if there are resources unemployed. Does an increase in any form of economic activity have the same effect?

9. Explain how changes in the monetary policy of a country may influence its balance of payments.

TEST 2

1. Investment made equal to the amount of planned savings will ensure full employment. Do you agree? If not, what further measures must be taken to achieve this?

2. What is an indifference map? Use such a map to show the effect on the supply of labour of a rise in wages.

3. What do you understand by cross-elasticity? How would you use it to measure monopoly power?

4. How is price determined in the long period?

5. It pays a firm to pay high wages. Discuss.

6. What effect has a decrease in the marginal efficiency of capital upon the rate of interest and upon national income?

7. Comment upon the view that the payment of interest on the national debt represents a transfer payment, as distinct from part of the national income.

8. Argue the case for a tax based on expenditure instead of income.

9. Write short notes on *three* of the following:

    (*a*) The "warranted" rate of growth.
    (*b*) Arc elasticity.
    (*c*) The "cobweb" theorem.
    (*d*) National income and expenditure matrix.
    (*e*) Flexible exchange rates.

TEST 3

1. What would be the effect of a rise in the price of gold upon the monetary reserves of central banks?

2. What taxes would you propose or increase, and what taxes would you avoid, if you wished to add to the income of the government with a minimum of discouragement to the economic activity of the taxpayer?

3. What is the national income? Show its relationship with the total domestic expenditure.

4. What is the effect upon the price of a commodity and the amount purchased when the buyer is a monopsonist?

5. What is the effect upon investment if there is an increase in demand for a particular commodity?

6. How do savings affect the national income?

7. How are prices determined under conditions of oligopoly?

8. What determines the rate of interest? Is there any relationship between the rate of interest and the level of national income?

9. Write short notes on *three* of the following:

    (*a*) The "kinked" demand curve.
    (*b*) The marginal efficiency of investment.
    (*c*) The accelerator.
    (*d*) The Triffin plan.
    (*e*) The marginal propensity to import.

TEST 4

1. Is it true that the elasticity of demand depends wholly upor the presence or absence of substitutes for the goods concerned?

(C.I.S.)

2. What is the "world liquidity problem?"   (*C.I.S.*)

3. Discuss the relative merits of open-market operations and of changes in the liquidity ratio of commercial banks as methods of controlling the quantity of bank credit.   (*C.I.S.*)

4. Will oligopoly be likely to result in stable, or in fluctuating prices?   (*C.I.S.*)

5. It is sometimes argued that steeply progressive taxation discourages enterprise in the more wealthy taxpayers and responsibility in the less wealthy. Discuss this proposition.

(*C.I.S.*)

6. Discuss the difficulties of defining and measuring the real national income of a country.   (*C.I.S.*)

7. "Wages depend on productivity; but productivity does not depend on wages." Consider this statement.   (*C.I.S.*)

8. How can economic growth be assisted?   (*C.I.S.*)

9. Write notes on *two* of the following:

   (*a*) The capital market.

   (*b*) Economies of scale.

   (*c*) Vertical integration of industry.

(*C.I.S.*)

TEST 5

1. Why are the main British and American producers of motor-cars large and few?   (*C.I.S.*)

2. Compare the advantages and disadvantages of fixed exchange rates and of flexible exchange rates.   (*C.I.S.*)

3. Examine the dictum that the only effective remedy for an adverse balance of payments is deflation.   (*C.I.S.*)

4. "It is no more true to say that wages are determined by the marginal productivity of labour than that prices are determined by costs of production." Discuss.   (*C.I.S.*)

5. Does it pay a firm which is losing money to stay in existence?

(*C.I.S.*)

6. How does a well-developed banking system assist economic activity?   (*C.I.S.*)

7. "One of the greatest evils of modern society is price-cutting." "The benefits of economic progress must be passed on to the consumer in lower prices." Consider these statements. (*C.I.S.*)

8. Write notes on *two* of the following:

   (*a*) The National Debt.

   (*b*) The optimum firm.

   (*c*) Oligopoly.

   (*d*) The accelerator.

(*C.I.S.*)

TEST 6

In the following test, *four* questions are required to be answered in *three* hours.

1. Explain why usually more of a commodity is bought when the price is lowered. On what does the amount of the increase depend? (*B.Sc.(Soc). University of London*)

2. "In perfect competition the firm's marginal cost curve is its supply curve." Explain. (*B.Sc.(Soc). University of London*)

3. "A firm will go out of business if it does not recover its costs." Discuss. (*B.Sc.(Soc). University of London*)

4. Britain is often said to have a balance of payments problem. What is this problem and how might it be solved? (*B.Sc.(Soc). University of London*)

5. Show the significance of savings and investment in employment theory. (*B.Sc.(Soc). University of London*)

6. What are the chief factors that account for year-to-year changes in the national income? (*B.S.(Soc). University of London*)

TEST 7

In the following test, *four* questions are required to be answered in *three* hours.

1. Explain the meaning of the acceleration principle and discuss the conditions under which you would expect to find it operative. (*B.Sc.(Econ). University of London*)

2. Explain how it is possible for the reduction of a duty on a particular commodity to lead to an increase in the total revenue yielded by the duty. Give examples. (*B.Sc.(Econ). University of London*)

3. "Super-normal profits are a rent and may be taxed away without affecting business enterprise." Discuss. (*B.Sc.(Econ). University of London*)

4. Compare the rôle of gold under (*a*) the gold standard, and (*b*) the International Monetary Fund. (*B.Sc.(Econ). University of London*)

5. On what factors does the size of an industry and the number of firms comprising it depend? (*B.Sc.(Econ). University of London*)

6. In what ways has the use of indifference curves aided economic analysis? (*B.Sc.(Econ). University of London*)

INDEX